# What people are saying about Forgiving Forward...

▶▶

*"Why another book on forgiveness? If that question is not answered you may miss one of the most significant values of Forgiving Forward. A part of the answer to that question lies in the fact that the great emphases on forgiveness must be massaged, unfolded and applied in such a manner as to radically change lifestyles and undergird the sustainability of forgiveness. This is one of the greatest strengths of this book. This is not just another book on the subject but one that is likely to make others you have read more palatable, practical and explainable. The book is well done, simply put and makes forgiveness a memorable experience as well as tend toward a stable character trait in the reader. Well done, Bruce and Toni! Thanks! To the reader: Welcome to the Forgiveness Revolution!"*

—**Jack Taylor**, president,
Dimension Ministries, Melbourne, Florida

*"Do you want an answer to addictions and interpersonal conflict? Read this book! Do you desire to lead others to the forgiveness path? Read this book! Forgiving Forward is honest, practical and life changing. I highly recommend it!"*

—**Linda Dillow**, author,
*What's it Like to be Married to Me?* and
*Calm My Anxious Heart*

*Bruce and Toni Hebel have a powerful message for followers of
Christ: Forgiveness is not only central to our salvation, but also
to our ongoing walk with Christ. Indeed, many of our deepest
struggles can be traced to lack of forgiveness. Forgiving Forward
shows us how to practically apply scriptural teachings on forgiveness, and illustrates these principles with compelling stories."*

—**Dave Boehi**, senior editor, *FamilyLife*

*"With passion and a fierce determination born of those who
personally know the need, Bruce and Toni invite us to join the
Forgiveness Revolution. Through words that are biblically sound
and deeply profound, Bruce and Toni lay out the cause and explain
how embracing it will heal the church's most flagrant bleeding
wound. This is the right book in the right season with the right
message...it should be required reading material for every follower
of Jesus Christ."*

—**Lorraine Pintus**, international speaker,
writing coach, and author of
*Jump Off the Hormone Swing.*

*When I first met Bruce and Toni Hebel, they had been freshly
bruised by the people they had sought to bless. They took their
pain to God, drank in His grace, and discovered the life-changing
power of forgiveness. Upon discovering the sweet joy of a
bitter-free heart, Bruce and Toni set out to start a revolution of
forgiveness. Their book invites us into a life-changing mission—helping others forgive. Laden with real life stories and real spiritual
truths, Forgiving Forward is inspiring and instructive. It'll not
only set you free, it'll help you lead the ones you love to freedom.*

—**Alan D. Wright**, senior pastor
Reynolda Church, author of
*Lover of My Soul* and *Free Yourself, Be Yourself,*
teacher, nationally broadcast radio program,
"*Sharing the Light with Alan Wright.*"

*"Bruce and Toni turn our hearts towards the single issue that can keep any Christian, family, or community from realizing their full potential in Christ—unforgiveness. You'll learn how to help others discover our right, reason and responsibility to forgive others by releasing a debt that has actually already been paid. Forgiving Forward assigns to each us of the most liberating task of freeing others and ourselves from the bondage of unforgiveness. I'm glad to be part of the Revolution!"*

—**Robert W. Crummie**,
president, Carver College,
pastor, Mt. Calvary Missionary Baptist Church

*"Forgiveness is biblical. It is also essential. Forgiving Forward makes the case for the former and shows you how to do the latter. A practical guide to this Christian virtue, Bruce and Toni Hebel have provided a valuable resource for bringing 'Gospel-healing' to the body of Christ."*

—**Daniel L. Akin**, president,
Southeastern Baptist Theological Seminary

*"Reading through the book written by Bruce and Toni Hebel is like allowing God to comb through your soul and surface hidden hurts, bitterness and then lead to the freedom of forgiveness. The need to forgive and to be forgiven is perhaps the most universal and healing topic known to man. Bruce and Toni do a great job presenting this topic from a Biblical point of view in a way that is both engaging and liberating. I especially love the statement, "Conventional wisdom says there are certain things that are unforgivable and unrecoverable. But conventional wisdom often undervalues the power of the cross." This is a book of great hope for all who read it."*

—**Eddie Lyons**, senior pastor,
Highstreet Baptist Church, Springfield, MO

*As we mature, we come to realize that Jesus lives His Eternal Life through us. Forgiving Forward helps us understand how we can cooperate with what He wants to do through us here and now in the ongoing revolution.*

—*James Hicks, Ph.D*
president, Center for Growth and Change

# FORGIVING FORWARD
## Unleashing the Forgiveness Revolution

# BRUCE *and* TONI HEBEL

REGENERATING
LIFE PRESS

FORGIVING FORWARD
*Regenerating Life Press*
P.O. Box 1355
Fayetteville GA 30214

Every story in this book is an account of an actual event. No composite anecdotes or other fiction techniques have been used. However, details in some stories have been modified slightly to improve readability and the names of some of the individuals have been changed to protect their privacy.

Unless otherwise noted, all Scripture quotations taken from the New American Standard Bible® Copyright © 1960, 1962, 1963, 1971, 1972, 1973, 1975, 1977, 1995 by The Lockman Foundation. Used by permission.

Scripture quotations marked (NIV) are taken from the Holy Bible, NEW INTERNATIONAL VERSION®. Copyright © 1973, 1978, 1984, by International Bible Society. Used by permission of Zondervan Publishing House. All rights reserved.

ISBN 978-1-936983-00-1
Copyright © 2011, Bruce and Toni Hebel

Printed in the United States of America.

*Writing Coach:* Kathy Carlton Willis, Kathy Carlton Willis
    Communications, kathycarltonwillis.com
*Cover Design:* Randy Drake, Randy Drake Design,
    randydrakedesign.com
*Cover Photography:* Aldrich Lim, aldrichlim.com
*Author Photograph:* Shana Keaton
*Book Designer:* Debbie Patrick, Vision Run, visionrun.com

To Aaron, Andrew and Amy.
Thanks for choosing to join the Revolution
rather than become casualties of the War.

# Contents
▶▶

# Foreword
▶▶

*Could it be that we've missed something?* Something deeply necessary to our journey towards wholeness? Is there a reason why peace tends to feel elusive; frayed at the edges? Is this truly the 'abundant life' Christ clothed himself in flesh for? Died for? Could forgiveness really be such an essential part of finding the crux of this 'abundant life'—the life Christ wanted us to experience this side of heaven as well? After years of ministry, I have never been more convinced of the centrality of forgiveness in the gospel story—in *our* story. Nor have I been more convinced that Christ's teaching on forgiveness is largely and wildly… *misunderstood.*

Forgiveness tends to be an obscure principle in today's world—even among those who follow Christ. We all know the familiar saying, "time heals all wounds," and yet we watch those around us shrivel from the pain of distant wounds that still seem to bleed fresh, raw, and unhealed. Perhaps you are one of the many who wonder why the blood of the cross has covered and removed all of *your* sins—but *you* (or loved ones in your life) cannot seem to unfasten the pain and heartache from wounds caused by those who have sinned against *you*. Take heart, friend, for nestled deep within

Christ's ancient teaching—and within the pages of this book— is a living, recreating truth that has the power to heal and restore that which has been broken. It is a truth that allows enemies to be blessed, the wounded to rise again and pray for those who have wronged them; a truth that allows peace to reign. It is no accident that you hold this book in your hands.

*Forgiving Forward* is an engaging, authentic dialogue teeming with real life stories and transformative Biblical teaching that examines the path of forgiveness throughout the redemptive story between God and humankind: climaxing at the cross, and continuing in the body of Christ's believers. Bruce and Toni have experienced the healing power of forgiveness—both in their own lives, and as they have served as the catalysts of forgiveness in the lives of *hundreds* of others. They understand the complexities of the inner world of the heart, and operate as wonderful spiritual companions on the journey towards experiencing personal forgiveness, as well as being trained in how to assist others in experiencing this same freedom. Their insight is refreshing and honest. The *Forgiveness Revolution* recognizes that when we pray for God's kingdom to exist on earth 'as it is in heaven' we are asking for—inviting—a kingdom that "sets the captives free."

*Forgiving Forward* is such an important book because the need for forgiveness is universal. It is universal because we live and breathe in a fallen world. Eden has been lost. Perfection has been displaced by imperfection, and as a result, wounds are an inevitable part of life. We hurt others—intentionally or unintentionally. Others hurt us—intentionally or unintentionally. Identical to biological wounds that occur in the physical realm, heart-wounds that occur in the spiritual realm must be treated properly so that infection does not spread throughout the inner being. It's shocking how much seemingly disproportionate havoc a small wound left untreated can cause. Have you ever stopped to wonder what the consequences are of a neglected, unforgiving heart? If it is the will of God for us experience and embody forgiveness, would it not stand to reason that He has revealed the means by which we find this radical love that he speaks of? Could it be that there are hidden gems pressed ever so slightly beneath the surface of familiar scriptures that we've not quite seen before?

Won't you join Bruce and Toni as they seek to bring about the transformation of the inner life: from unrest to *peace*, and from bondage to *freedom*. The truth within the margins of these pages bursts at the seams and is a truth that must to be listened to—meditated upon—ingested deep within. It is a "truth that sets us free." Is that not why Christ came? Come discover the reason why Christ made forgiveness such a primary concern in the Lord's Prayer: "Forgive us our sins, *as we forgive those who sin against us.*" My challenge to you is read slowly, open your heart wide, and prepare to watch God's kingdom draw near to earth... A kingdom longing to pour forth its richest blessings; a kingdom where "those who have been forgiven much, love much."


## *Bruce Wilkinson*
www.BruceWilkinson.com
www.Facebook.com/LastingLifeChange

# Preface
▸▸

The book you hold in your hand is a result of a lifelong project that started two years ago. Let me try to explain.

Growing up in a pastor's home and having been in ministry for over 30 years, I have encountered many hurting people. "Hurting people hurt people" is a phrase I know well. Over the years, I observed my father get hurt in ministry and I've also been betrayed, abandoned and deeply wounded. The same is true for Toni and our kids. We have suffered the pain that unforgiveness brings and have experienced the peace that comes through forgiving. We've had many opportunities to give up on people, to give up on ourselves, to give up on the church and to give up on God, but we chose not to. Why? Because we have been taught the truth of forgiveness.

The message of forgiveness is so powerful because it is central to the message of the cross. This lesson is not one that is learned out of good times and easy circumstances. The only way to learn forgiveness is to have something to forgive. In talking with the pastoral counseling team at Focus on the Family, they said that our story was one of the worst they have seen and that most people would have "left the ministry by now." Why have we been able to keep going? Three reasons: First, the Grace of God! He has been so faithful to us especially in our time of deepest pain. Second, both of our fathers drilled into us the determination to "not quit." Third, we have learned the power of forgiveness. With the Grace of God sustaining us, and something inside that would not let us quit, we discovered forgiveness was our only way to personal freedom.

So you see, my whole life has been leading to this message of the book you're holding in your hands. But, until two years ago, I had no intention of writing a book. It was not a childhood dream nor had it made it's way onto my bucket list. But sometimes God prepares us to do things we do not know we are going to do. Through divine orchestration, Dr. Bruce Wilkinson taught a series of messages that became the book *You Were Born For This* in the Spring of 2009. He was with us at our church, ReGen Fellowship, for 19 nights over a six-week period, during which time we became friends. As teachers often do, we spent time sharing with each other the things God had been teaching us. One of the subjects we discussed was the message of forgiveness. In my conversations with Bruce, he assured me that the multiple betrayals in ministry were God's gift to us to prepare or train us for our greater ministry. The greater ministry for us is to teach the freedom of forgiveness to a broader audience. He then looked at me and said, "You need to write a book on forgiveness." I responded with, "You are 'Bruce the writer' and I am 'Bruce the reader,' you write it." He laughed, but was undeterred in his insistence that we were to write this book. Without his encouragement to both Toni and me, *Forgiving Forward* would not be a reality.

We believe in the church as Jesus designed it. We believe the message of forgiveness is the core message that the church is to communicate. We also believe that unforgiveness may be the most significant blockage to the church being as fruitful as God wants it to be. It is the source of most church conflicts. Too often we hear, in the broader church of America, stories of leaders who have been hurt by the church and churchgoers hurt by their leaders. I have been on both sides of that equation. I have also seen and experienced the torment that refusing to forgive brings and the breakthrough of peace and freedom when forgiveness is given. I am committed to the church and to helping it to learn this central truth. As I researched, I was shocked at the relatively small volume of material available to help the church in this message that is so core to the Gospel. The scarcity of material training the church on how to help others forgive is one of the compelling reasons for us to put this message on paper.

As we have worked out these principles in our own lives, God has brought us into contact with many wounded pastors, ministry leaders and people on the street that are in torment because of unforgiveness. It has been amazing to witness significant supernatural breakthroughs. Toni and I are regularly finding opportunities to help people we meet work through this message of *Forgiving Forward*. We have received incredible joy in helping others forgive. In fact, nothing has brought more joy than helping someone else find the peace that comes from forgiving—except maybe hearing that the person we've helped is now helping someone else to forgive.

Something miraculous happened on December 28, 1979, Bruce Hebel and Toni Park became one. Since our wedding day, we've had a very blessed connection as husband and wife. We truly are one. What has hurt me has impacted her and what has hurt her has impacted me. We both have our unique abilities and gifts; the strength of us is *us*. However, it is difficult to write a book in the first person plural voice. We have chosen to write it from my (Bruce) voice. The *I's* refer to Bruce and the *We's* refer to Bruce and Toni. The strategy we use in writing is best defined as collaboration. I did the initial writing and Biblical research. Toni wrote some of the stories. After I was done with the chapter she would read it and edit it. We would go back and forth until we were both satisfied with the chapter, and ultimately the book.

There are a couple of things that would be helpful for you to understand as you read this book. First, when we refer to a "miracle," we are referring to a specific definition of the word miracle. We define a miracle as "any time God moves in time and space to meet someone's need in such a way that they know God did it." We recognize that there are many types of miracles as well as many definitions of the word miracle. We have chosen not to spend a lot of time explaining this concept of miracle in the book. We derived it from our interaction with Dr. Wilkinson and from his book, *You Were Born For This*. We encourage you, if you've not already done so, to read that work to gain a better understanding of the miracle delivery process.

Second, the stories in this book are true. While we could have found many stories from people's lives in other books, we chose to limit our stories to the ones that we were directly involved with. These stories are either of people that we coached through forgiveness or are stories of people that were coached through forgiveness by someone we trained. We want you to know that what we are teaching is not theory to us, it is life to us. We have received permission to share the stories with you and many of the names have been changed to protect the forgiven. We have discovered that once people have been truly set free through this transformational message, they become passionate about helping others find that same freedom.

We believe that the truths of radical forgiveness may be the most important message for the world today. Everyone needs to become expert forgivers, whether it's pastors, church leaders, the people in the pews or the people on the streets. It is a universal message with a universal impact. It is a message that the Holy Spirit has given to us. It is a message that God wants all of us to live and share. *The Forgiveness Revolution* has begun—it must be unleashed!

Bruce (for Toni)

# PART ONE

# Forgiving Forward:
# The Mandate

▶▶

CHAPTER ONE

# Calling All Revolutionaries
▸▸

W hat if I told you that you could be a part of a revolution that radically rescues people from a life filled with torture? What if I told you the people you would be setting free live all around you? Would you be interested?

I've always been intrigued by revolutionaries. You know, people who make a difference. I admire men and women who, at great personal risk, fearlessly rescue someone from imminent danger and oppression. Growing up I secretly wanted to be someone like Paul Revere or Sir Lancelot or any character played by John Wayne.

I'm amazed at the popularity of the movie Braveheart, the story of William Wallace and how he led a revolt to overthrow England's tyrannical reign over his beloved Scotland. Personally, I would have put this in the "guy movie" category. Yet my daughter and her college friends rank it as one of their favorites. I recently spoke at a women's shelter and recovery center where I referenced Braveheart in my talk to them. The overwhelming response was, "I love that movie." Why is that? My guess is, William Wallace willingly sacrificed everything to free his beloved countrymen from the tyranny of Longshanks, King Edward I. There is something deep within all of us that longs to make the difference Wallace made. Does this ring true? If so, this revolution is for you.

You see, I'm a recruiter for a revolution that desperately needs your help. We're looking for men and women who are willing to make a difference. And guess what? You don't have to relocate. The need is everywhere. You and I encounter people every single day who are tormented by old wounds and long to be free. If you will join the Forgiveness Revolution, you can help them. Guaranteed! And it's not as hard as you may think.

### How We Joined the Revolution

We joined the revolution at my parent's kitchen table in February of 2006. My wife, Toni, and I made the 400-mile trek from Atlanta to Paducah, Kentucky to help with a bathroom remodeling project. (Okay, for those who know me, Toni did the faux painting, and I did my best Tim "the tool man" Taylor imitation.) But for the story to make sense, I need to give you some background.

First, my Dad and I had a great relationship. No "father wounds" for me. (Maybe there were a couple of bruises, but no real wounds.) I am blessed. He was a retired pastor who had served in churches for over 50 years. Since I followed his footsteps and became a pastor, we always found lots to talk about. I had great respect for him and he always made sure I knew how proud he was of me.

The second thing you need to know is, I had just gone through a deep cleansing period with God. While on a sabbatical, I had dealt with an old wound from a previous church experience that had festered into a deceptive bitterness, which tormented me for over a year. It took a sabbatical, a counselor, a three-day personal prayer and fasting retreat and R.T. Kendall's book "Total Forgiveness" to set me free. It was pretty amazing. When I returned home I shared my miracle story with my wife and kids, who had also been deeply hurt by this church wound. The unexpected happened. My entire family was also set free through forgiveness. We spent an entire day, 10 hours, forgiving those who had hurt us, including burning incriminating documents and deleting emails related to the wound. These acts of cleansing led to each one of us giving and receiving forgiveness among ourselves for past wounds in our family. We were forever changed and healed. So, of course, my story of forgiveness became a topic of conversation during our visit with my folks as we caught up between coats of paint.

On our last morning there, Mom was out running an errand. Toni and I sat at the table after breakfast sipping coffee and tea while chatting with my dad. Papa was a great pastor and normally pretty upbeat despite struggling with heart disease and diabetes. But on this particular day, He was kvetching about a couple of people. He wasn't saying anything real mean, but bitterness leaked out of his words. He couldn't see it, but we could. It was obvious. These wounds were eating him alive.

At this point, I heard a voice inside my spirit say "speak into your father about forgiveness." It wasn't an audible voice, but it was very clear. I immediately went into a high-speed debate in my head. It went something like this.

"Lord, you know he is my dad, right?"

"I know. I was there when both of you were born. Speak into his life!"

"But sons do not correct their parents," I said.

"They do if I tell them too. Speak into him!"

"Well, if I knew it was really You, Lord, I would. How do I know it's You?" I questioned.

"You know it's Me, quit stalling and speak into your dad's heart. It will be alright."

"This may upset him," I responded. "Who do you prefer to be upset with you, him or Me?"

"Good point!" I replied.

"Just trust Me."

"OK Lord, here goes…"

(I know it may sound weird, but that's how my conversations often go with God.)

So, swallowing hard, I said, "Papa, you know I love you and you can do whatever you wish with this. I hope I don't make you mad, but it sounds to me like you are bitter at Don and John. You've been friends with Don for over fifty years. I'm sure he did not mean to hurt you and he probably doesn't even know that he did. You've known John for over thirty-five years. He was like a son to you, and Carla (his wife) was like my third sister. I think it might be time to forgive and let them off the hook. You can do what you want to, but that's what I sense I am supposed to say to you." And then I braced for his response.

What happened next was remarkable. Without any hesitation, my 76-year-old father immediately responded by saying, "Son, I stand rebuked. You are right. I need to forgive and reconcile with both of them. Will you pray with me?" Papa then left his kitchen chair and kneeled with his face to the floor. As we prayed together, tears welled up in his eyes. He repented of his unforgiveness and forgave both of his friends from his heart. As soon as he finished, I noticed his countenance had changed and his spirit was at peace. It took great effort for him to stand up from that praying posture, but as he did, he wrapped his arms around me—weeping and thanking me. We embraced for quite some time. Then he proceeded to put a CD in his CD player to worship the Lord who had just forgiven him. Papa was free!

While most people who know Papa might not have noticed his bitterness, we did. He needed to forgive, but he needed help.

## A SURPRISING ANSWER TO AN AGE-OLD QUESTION

And to think, I might have missed it. I mean, come on. Who talks to his 76-year-old dad like that? Speak when spoken to, right? When someone wants your opinion or help for that matter, they will ask for it, otherwise keep it to yourself. Isn't that how it works? After all, I am not my brother's, or in my case, father's keeper, am I?

This is an important question. If you listen to the voices of our culture you will hear, "Of course not. I am only responsible for me. Everyone makes their own choices and their own way. I stay out of everyone else's business and they had better stay out of mine!" "Mind your own business" is the motto we often live by. That certainly was the assumption behind Cain's challenge to God in Genesis 4. But what if that is not the correct answer? What if we see that God's view is exactly the opposite of what we often think?

**God's real answer to Cain was "Yes, you really are your brother's keeper!"**

It's a familiar story. Adam and Eve had two sons, Cain and Abel. In short, the story goes like this. Cain was a farmer and Abel, a shepherd. In the course of time, both brothers brought an offering to the Lord, Cain from his crops and Abel from his flocks. For reasons that are much debated, the Lord accepted Abel's offering and rejected Cain's. Cain fumed about it, and God confronted him and warned him of the risk of his self-focus. Ignoring God's warning, Cain killed his brother.

Then God asked a question that He fully knew the answer to (so like God!). "Where is your brother Abel?" Cain tried to dodge the question with a question (so like humans!).

"I do not know," he lied. "Am I my brother's keeper?"

Then God said, "Oh yeah, you're right. What was I thinking? Sorry for the question, Cain, old friend. We're cool!" If you listen to what seems to be a prevailing mindset, that's what you might expect to hear. But that is exactly the opposite of what God said. In so many words God told Cain he was not only responsible for his own attitude, but also the safety of his brother. God's real answer to Cain was "Yes, you really *are* your brother's keeper!"

The Bible says a lot about us helping other people, particularly when they are in crisis. On more than one occasion in Genesis,

Abraham rescued Lot when he was in trouble. The Old Testament prophets routinely confronted the kings, often uninvited. David clearly did not see Nathan's rebuke about his adultery and murder coming. King Ahab was never happy to see Elijah.

The New Testament contains several "brother's keepers" passages as well. For example, 2 Timothy 2:2 tells us that we are to take what we learn and pass it on to others, who will pass it on as well. Likewise, Colossians 1:28 states that the goal of ministry is to proclaim Christ by admonishing and instructing people. I don't know about you, but while I need admonishing at times, I rarely invite it. 2 Corinthians 5:17-19 tells us we have been given the "ministry of reconciliation" and Paul is begging people to be reconciled with God. In fact, Jesus came into the world uninvited and very much underappreciated, but He still came!

**From time to time we all need a helping hand. This is true of 100 percent of us.**

One of the key chapters in the Bible that speaks to the subject of forgiveness is Matthew 18. In verses 15-17, Jesus gives the process in which we are to confront a brother who is in sin. The often ignored process involves going in private, and if that doesn't work, taking one or two others along. If the small group intervention isn't successful, we are to get the church involved.

One of the clearest "brother's keepers" passages is Galatians 6:1-2 which reads, *"Brethren, even if anyone is caught in any trespass, you who are spiritual, restore such a one in a spirit of gentleness; each one looking to yourself, so that you too will not be tempted. Bear one another's burdens, and thereby fulfill the law of Christ."* There is something unsettling to me about this. It is way outside my comfort zone. What Paul is saying is, if we see someone trapped, we are responsible to help get them out.

The imagery of the word *caught* is that of someone caught in a trap. Think of a bear trap. A bear trap is designed in such a way that if one unsuspectingly steps into it, he is not able to extricate himself without help. It takes someone standing with a foot on each end of the trap to release it. Obviously, if one foot is caught in the jaws of the trap, you would be one foot short to open the trap. Someone else must take the initiative to come to your aid to set you free.

From time to time we all need a helping hand. This is true of 100 percent of us. It is universal. There are certain struggles (unforgiveness is one of them) which are almost impossible to overcome alone. Often times we are the last to recognize our own problem areas. Some of the most painful—and valuable— times in my life have been when a friend took the risk of confronting me about something he saw in me. As difficult as those conversations were, they were incredible growth points in my life. There have also been times when I have had to help others with their blind spots. Remember, blind spots are called "blind" for a reason.

This process of helping people is tricky. I have seen this go terribly wrong because some people resemble the old *Leadership Journal* cartoon of a couple of grumpy old men in dark suits walking together as one says to the other, "Ever had one of those days when you just had to rebuke somebody?" People who are struggling with something can smell a judgmental spirit from a mile away. Galatians 6:1 tells us this is reserved for people who are in a good place with God personally and who are sensitive to the fact that tomorrow they could be in a similar predicament. There is no room for looking down our spiritual noses at someone in any of this. Pride just gets in the way and short circuits the process.

### A Hidden Cancer

My friend James is brilliant at gracious confrontation. James is a counselor by training and a friend by calling. He helped me deal with my sin of unforgiveness in January of 2006. He was always gentle and most of the time came through the back door, using one of his stories to deal with an issue. Sitting in his den, wearing black jeans, boots and a red shirt from a Mexican restaurant in

Texas, James would say, "Now, I'm not one to judge because I may have broken all of the Ten Commandments in one way or another, plus some, but I think you might want to think about..." James, in his hyperbole, recognized that we all have the capacity to sin and mess up at any time. He has an amazing sensitivity to the Holy Spirit and to people, which puts them at ease so he can help them overcome their struggle. He certainly created a safe and non-judgmental environment in which he gently guided me to discover how self-destructive my unforgiveness had become. I would not have found freedom without his help.

You see, unforgiveness can be one of the most deceptive and deadly traps we fall into. It has been said that, "Bitterness is the poison we drink hoping someone else dies." Every time I repeat this quote to someone, the response is "Whoa! That is so right!" And it is. *Bitterness is to a heart wound what infection is to a flesh wound.* Personally, I am very prone to infection so I have to take extra precautions whenever I get a cut or scrape. If the wound is kept clean and medicated, I have no problem. But, if the wound is ignored, infection sets in which increases the pain and extends the recovery time. I still have a scar on my left hand from a simple burn I received when I was a kid because I allowed it to get infected. You see it doesn't matter who caused the original injury. If I do not properly care for the wound, the infection is my fault. And if things go unattended too long, outside help (i.e. a doctor) is required.

The same thing is true with a heart wound; only the consequences can be much greater. If we do not cleanse the wound by forgiving, bitterness can quietly set in without us realizing it. We will examine the signs of unforgiveness and bitterness in Chapter Seven. What is important to know at this point is that the signs of bitterness are easy to detect—in someone else. Not so easy in ourselves. Sometimes the infection becomes a cancerous growth buried deep within us; yet, left unaddressed, it will only get worse. Outside detection is often crucial to the process.

In the fall of 1993, my buddy James bought an old Harley

Davidson motorcycle for the purpose of fixing it up and selling it in the spring of '94. He had a pretty good strategy: buy when they are selling and sell when they are buying. But hey, "you gotta test drive it before you sell it, right?" James thought so. So off he went with a friend to the North Georgia Mountains. Two friends, two bikes and a gorgeous spring day. What's not to like? However, somewhere near Dahlonega, the Harley's wheels suddenly slid sideways. James and his freshly refurbished treasure both skidded down the side of the mountain. The next thing he knew, he was waking up in the hospital.

The medical personnel at the hospital were concerned about internal injuries, so they sent James to the radiology department for a CT scan. He had a serious and pragmatic objection to the procedure. The CT scan required that he raise both arms over his head and hold them still during the entire scan. The problem was he could not raise his right arm without excruciating pain because his shoulder had been separated. James, in his inimitable way, actually talked his way out of the test. Not surprising.

As the young lady, who served as his gurney driver, wheeled him out of radiology, James heard a familiar song playing over the intercom. It was the theme to "The Cotton Patch Gospel," a stage play depicting the Gospel of Matthew re-written in 20th century Georgia. It was very creatively written and reset Atlanta as Jerusalem, Valdosta as Nazareth, and Gainesville as Bethlehem. The lyrics begin like this, *"Something's going on in Gainesville, wonder what it could be. Something's going on in Gainesville, come on down and see."*

"That's a great song they're playing," James said to the orderly. He had seen the Cotton Patch Gospel on more than one occasion and really liked the music.

"What song, Mr. Hicks? There is no music playing," she responded.

"You don't hear any music?" He insisted.

"No, sir. They don't play music in the halls of this hospital."

"Where are we?" Concerned and confused he looked around.

"You are in the hospital, Mr. Hicks. You have a head injury," she replied, as she thought to herself, "Poor man. His head injury has him hearing things."

James hesitated then exhaled hard. "I know I am in the hospital. The last thing I remember before I woke up here on this bed is sliding down an embankment near Dahlonega. I just don't know which hospital they brought me to. What city is this hospital in?"

"You are in the Gainesville Hospital, Mr. Hicks." The gurney squeaked down the hallway toward his room.

"Something's going on in Gainesville, wonder what it could be? Something's going on in Gainesville, come on down and see." He recounted the lyrics over again in his head.

"Wheel me back to the radiology room. We need to do this thing!"

At his suggestion, they used a towel to tie his arms above his head. James endured the pain and completed the CT scan. The radiologist said to him, "I don't know what it is you heard," Mr. Hicks, "but whatever it was, it may have just saved your life."

The CT scan revealed that James had renal cell carcinoma, a quiet form of kidney cancer which 80 percent of the time is not diagnosed until autopsy. The other 20 percent of the time it is discovered looking for something else. James is alive today because a trained eye looked under the surface to find the obscure.

Several questions are in the back of my mind. If James' cancer had not been diagnosed, who would have helped me learn to forgive? Would my wife and children have found the freedom of forgiving? What about my dad and the lives he touched? One person can impact so many.

We need more people who are trained to diagnose the signs of unforgiveness and attuned enough to sensitively guide people through the process of forgiving. My hope is that by reading this book, you will join the Forgiveness Revolution and that through you an exponential number of people will find peace and freedom by learning to live the forgiving lifestyle we call *Forgiving Forward.*

*Forgiving Forward* is important because all of us run into people every day who are deeply troubled by old wounds and who mistakenly blame their current misery on someone from their past. Many often continue to blame the person who wounded them for their pain without realizing that it is their harboring of bitterness that has kept their pain alive. As we will see in Chapter Two, unforgiveness is the cause of much, if not most, of the emotional pain and turmoil in our lives. The sad part is we hold the antidote and often don't even know it. The good news is I have seen people with unbelievable stories of abuse and betrayal set free when they chose to forgive.

### SARAH'S STORY

I recently received a call from a pastor friend who, while counseling one of his members, recognized the signs of unforgiveness in her. This pastor and I had just returned from a mission trip where I taught on "*Forgiving Forward.*" He asked if I would meet with her. I agreed and, at the arranged time, the three of us met in my pastor friend's office. At 59, Sarah's furrowed brow and grooved frown lines screamed pain like neon lights—she had been hurting for a very long time. I introduced myself and assured her I was there to help and, as my dad used to say, "I've been to two county fairs and a box supper!" I told her that nothing she said would shock me, and that anything she told me would not affect what I thought of her. It would however, affect how I helped her. She relaxed and began to open up and tell her story.

What she described to me was one of the most appalling stories I've ever heard. The violation she endured was both unimaginable and sickening. At three years old, her parents repeatedly sold her into prostitution to a friend of her father's. Even though it all started fifty-six years ago, she recounted every detail, including the clothes she and the man wore, what he smelled like, what the car looked like and the surroundings where the violations took

**Love presses in and pays the price to set someone free.**

place. I thought to myself, this is going to be the test, Lord. If she is set free today, the Forgiveness Revolution will be for real. By the grace of God, two hours later at the end of our time together, she repented of her unforgiveness and forgave her parents and the man who violated her in such a horrific way.

I asked Sarah how she felt and if anything had changed. She said, "I can't believe it. I am really tired, but my heart is calm." Using her hands to illustrate, she continued. "For as long as I can remember, my heart felt like someone was constantly wringing it and squeezing it. It has never been at peace before. Now it is at peace." And we could see it. The change in her countenance was unmistakable. Forgiveness works. Sarah was free. But she needed help to get to that point —a midwife of sorts—to assist with the process. Her sensitive pastor observed the signs of unforgiveness and took action by requesting my assistance in escorting her into the Forgiveness Revolution. Together we helped Sarah find peace. I followed up with her pastor a couple of weeks later and asked how she was doing. He reported that when she went home that night, for the first time, she was able to sleep without nightmares. Not one disturbing dream has interrupted her sleep since. She is at peace.

A final observation on Galatians 6:2. When we help people with struggles, when we become our "brother's keeper," so to speak, we are reflecting the love of Jesus. I once heard Chip Ingram define love as "giving someone what they need most, when they deserve it the least, at great personal sacrifice."[1] Often when people are trapped, they are like the proverbial lion with a thorn in it's paw. The thorn needs to come out, but the lion fights anyone who comes close enough to help. Yet love presses in and pays the price to set someone free. I think you will find the payoff is well worth it.

So how about it? Are you ready to consider joining the revolution? Maybe it has to start with you. Perhaps you will discover something you need to deal with. That's good. 100 percent of the human population has been hurt by someone. Therefore, every single one of us, without exception, at some time or another, needs to forgive someone. If there is a person or an event that nags at your heart, I hope this book helps you learn to forgive. When you do, I also hope you catch the Forgiveness Revolution and are challenged to *Forgive Forward*.

Oh, by the way, about my dad. Within two weeks of forgiving his friends, Papa met and reconciled with both of the men. And for the rest of his life he became a forgiveness evangelist. He talked to his doctors and the people in their offices about it. He shared it with his Lions Club buddies, and at church. He gave away copies of my *Forgiving Forward* sermons to anyone who would accept them and promoted R.T. Kendall's book, *Total Forgiveness*, everywhere he went. Set free, Papa wanted to help everyone he could to find the freedom he had experienced.

One last note; Papa passed away seventeen months after our breakfast table conversation. At Papa's request, Don and John, the men he forgave, both spoke at his memorial service. The Forgiveness Revolution has been unleashed.

## Chapter Two

# Unforgiveness Brings Torment: Guaranteed!

▶▶

Sometime ago our doorbell rang and we opened the door to a familiar, yet not so familiar face. Emma and her family had been a part of our lives for several years and we always knew her to be upbeat, full of life and a bit mischievous. But that night we greeted a different Emma. The eyes that normally danced with joy were filled with anguish. The bright smile was gone, replaced by a blank, emotionless face. Something was dreadfully wrong. "What's going on, Emma?" I asked.

"It doesn't really matter, Bruce. He hurt me so deeply that I have no heart anymore!" She looked to the floor as she shuffled her feet in despair.

Our son greeted Emma as she came in and said to himself, "This looks serious" and immediately went downstairs to his room, leaving us alone to talk with her.

We moved into our den where I sat down in my recliner, my wife on the couch and Emma in the red cushioned chair across from us. In the next two hours her heart (which she didn't think she had) poured itself out to us. A serious relationship with a young man just recently ended dramatically, leaving her feeling violated and betrayed—causing a deep wound. The betrayal went public when her boyfriend announced on Facebook™, for her and all her friends to see, that he was now in a relationship with another man. She was understandably devastated. Toni and I had watched this relationship blossom and were both surprised and saddened by the story Emma recounted. At this point, however, we were more concerned with what was going on inside of her. The signs of internal torment were easy to see. As we began to show her God's perspective on her situation and led her through the protocols for finding peace, the lights began to come on in her eyes. We witnessed an incredible transformation take place in her as

she bowed her head and tearfully forgave herself and her ex-boyfriend. When she looked up after praying, her tormented eyes and blank, emotionless face had been replaced with her animated dancing eyes and that 300-watt smile of hers. The old Emma we had known and loved was back.

**God expects forgiven people to forgive others.**

It was remarkable. In fact, when our son came back upstairs before she left, he immediately noticed the change from when she had first arrived. "What happened to you?" he asked her. "I found my heart!" she exclaimed.

Emma's story is a common one. Everyone, at some time or another, has been hurt and stung by betrayal and offense. It's universal. But not everyone's story has an ending like Emma's. It often takes years before someone finds the peace and release Emma found in one evening. Why does it seem to take forever to recover from emotional wounds? What is the key that unlocks the door to peace and freedom after we've been wounded? The answer is found in the very core of the Gospel message. The answer that set Emma free is forgiveness.

C.S Lewis said, "Everyone thinks forgiveness is a lovely idea, until they have something to forgive."[2] It certainly seems a lot easier to receive forgiveness than it is to extend it to those who have hurt us. Yet that is exactly what God desires of us. God expects forgiven people to forgive others. He is extremely serious about this, maybe more so than any other issue in our lives. He withholds His protection from us when we do not forgive, and He unleashes His protection when we do forgive. It is that important to Him. Make no mistake. It should be just as important for us.

### A SHOCKING REALIZATION

It was sobering to me when I first realized God has linked His forgiveness of us with our forgiveness of others. I have to confess I am not sure I like this point, but it is unavoidable in a careful study of the subject of forgiveness. The only part of The Lord's Prayer (Matthew 6:9-13), that Jesus gives immediate commentary on is the statement, *"And forgive us our debts as we have also forgiven our debtors."* Immediately after giving the model prayer, Jesus says that if we forgive others, our Father will forgive us. But if we do not forgive others, He will not forgive us. (Matthew 6:14-15) Notice the prayer isn't, "God, we will use Your model for forgiving when we forgive others." It is quite the opposite. We are to pray, *"God, use the way in which we forgive others as the standard You use to forgive us."* Ouch! I found that this isn't isolated to just this one passage. We find Mark 11:25-26 teaching the same truth. *"Whenever you stand praying, forgive, if you have anything against anyone, so that your Father who is in heaven will also forgive you your transgressions. But if you do not forgive, neither will your Father who is in heaven forgive your transgressions."*

> **God withholds His protection when we do not forgive, and He unleashes His protection when we do forgive.**

Does this mean that if I do not forgive, I cannot go to heaven? No, that is not what it means. In Y*ou Were Born For This,* Bruce Wilkinson explains it this way: "Now Jesus can't be referring here to what theologians call 'salvation forgiveness.' (This happens in Heaven and can't be earned—it is a gift from God to all who

believe in Jesus and His work on the cross as full payment for
their sins.) He's referring to the flow of God's pardon in our lives
on earth."[3] This distinction is contrasted in 1 John, where John,

**Unforgiveness robs us of peace and hinders our ability to hear God's voice.**

clearly speaking to followers of Jesus, says *"If we confess our sins, He is faithful and righteous to forgive us our sins and to cleanse us from all unrighteousness"* (1 John 1:9). He addresses it again in 1 John 2:1-2, *"My little children, I am writing these things to you so that you may not sin. And if anyone sins, we have an Advocate with the Father, Jesus Christ the righteous; and He Himself is the propitiation for our sins; and not for ours only, but also for those of the whole world."* While I am confident that there is *"no more condemnation for those in Christ Jesus"* (Romans 8:1), I also know I need daily cleansing for the things I do wrong on a daily basis to maintain the intimacy of my relationship with God. Unforgiveness robs us of peace and hinders our ability to hear God's voice. That is the forgiveness Jesus is referring to here. God is so serious about the importance of forgiveness that He links our willingness to forgive with His daily forgiveness of us.

As a pastor and seminary graduate, I am embarrassed to confess that for much of my life I somewhat blew past these verses without really thinking them through. I had wrestled with personal forgiveness and devoured *Total Forgiveness* and studied the subject quite thoroughly—or so I thought. I even taught a series on forgiveness when we started our new church. I really thought I had the topic of forgiveness nailed—until I heard Bruce Wilkinson teach on this subject. As I listened to Bruce unpack Jesus' parable in Matthew 18:21-35, the light bulbs went on in my head and I was shocked by what the Holy Spirit revealed to me. I couldn't believe what I discovered.

Peter begins the passage by asking Jesus the question, "How many times should I forgive someone? Would seven times be enough?" Peter knew the Pharisees said men were only required to forgive someone twice, but if they really wanted to be gracious, three times. So Peter thought he was being extremely magnanimous when he doubled the maximum plus one. His jaw must have dropped when Jesus set the bar at 490 times. In essence Jesus said there is no limit to how many times you forgive. (If someone is still keeping track when they get close to 490, they probably have not forgiven.) Jesus then uses a parable to make His point. I had read this parable numerous times and even taught on the topic. But it wasn't until that night that I grasped Jesus' main point.

A wealthy ruler decided to settle accounts with those who owed him money. One servant owed him 10,000 talents. That was an astronomical amount of money. The servant did not have the ability to repay the debt, so the ruler ordered the man and his family thrown in jail. The servant pleaded and said, "Please, please give me time. I will pay it back." (Notice he didn't ask for forgiveness; he asked for time.) The ruler's heart was moved with compassion and he forgave the man his debt. Just like that, the ruler personally absorbed the entire amount.

Let me work through the currency exchange for you. In Jesus' day, a *talent* equaled 60 *minas*. One *mina* was the equivalent of 3 months' wages. This means a *talent* was worth 180 months or 15 years' wages. Ten thousand talents would then equal 150,000 years worth of wages. "Please, please give me time?" 150,000 years—there's no way. Let's just say the median annual income in the U.S. is around $50,000. At that figure, 10,000 talents would roughly equal $7.5 billion in today's dollars. That's billion with a 'b'. When the ruler forgave the debt, his net-worth dropped 7.5 billion dollars and his servant's rose 7.5 billion dollars. What a gift. We might think the forgiven man would be grateful and be ready to forgive forward. And we would be wrong.

Incredibly, the forgiven man went and found someone who owed him money. The debt this time was 100 denarii. A denarius equaled one day's pay, so this debt was 100 days' wages—or roughly $17,000 in our current economy. Using the same appeal the forgiven man had used, the debtor begged for an opportunity to repay the loan. But this time, there was an actual chance he could feasibly pay it back. His debt was comparable to a car loan. Paying it off might take a few years, but it's doable. "Of course," the forgiven man said, "Take all the time you need." That's what he did, right? Unfortunately the forgiven man did just the opposite. He refused to forgive forward and threw his debtor into prison. Unbelievable!

Let's think about this. 150,000 years' wages versus one-third of a year's wages. That would be like $7.5 billion versus $17,000. A 450,000 to 1 ratio between what this man had been forgiven and what he was owed. While it would be virtually impossible to pay back $7.5 billion, it is entirely possible to repay $17,000. Incredibly, the one who had been forgiven an insurmountable obligation, refused to forgive a manageable debt.

As you might expect, the forgiven man's ingratitude and self-centeredness was noticed and denounced by everyone around. When the news got back to the wealthy ruler, he was justifiably incensed. He summoned the man, declared him to be a "wicked slave" and turned him over to be "tortured." The word "tortured" here is from the same root word as found in Luke 16:23 where the rich man of the "rich man and beggar Lazarus" fame, found himself in "torment" in Hades. This appears to be a stronger form of punishment than simply being put in debtor's prison. (Think William Wallace's last scene in *Braveheart*.) The torture was to continue until the entire debt was repaid.

After finishing the parable, Jesus then made a shocking statement in verse 35. "So shall my Heavenly Father also do to you, if each of you does not forgive his brother from your heart." Wow! You mean God in heaven is so serious about people forgiving others that He will allow us to be tormented when we refuse to forgive? When this first sunk in, (I can be a little slow) it sent shudders throughout my entire body. And look who He's talking to. He isn't talking to an unbelieving crowd. He is talking to Peter as the other disciples listened. This was His core team. These were the guys Jesus trained to take over for Him when He left. These were the guys to whom He would hand over the keys to the whole redemption strategy. These were His closest followers, the chosen few.

Now it is important to note what Jesus is *not* saying here. He is not saying they will lose their salvation. As stated earlier, He is not referring to eternal forgiveness, but rather the earthly relational benefits of His forgiveness. He's also not saying that God the Father tortures us. Indeed, the Father judges mankind and disciplines His children. The ruler in the parable did not torture the servant but turned him over to the tormenters who did. The Father simply withholds His protection from us and gives the enemy and his henchmen the legal authority to do the tormenting. Make no mistake; unforgiveness opens the door to a pretty miserable existence. I know. I learned this the hard way.

### LEARNING THE HARD WAY

Several years ago I was deeply wounded and betrayed at a church I worked for. It was a very dark and painful time for our family. At the lowest point in my life when I thought all hope was gone, God miraculously rescued us by taking us to a new place with a fresh start. The deliverance was quite remarkable. The timing was amazing. Yet in the middle of what we saw as a vindication, I neglected to forgive those involved from my heart. In particular, one man.

A few years later, through an unexpected encounter, the wound I thought was behind me was quietly reopened. The bitterness began to ooze out and I didn't notice. To make matters worse, current church happenings where I served reminded me of the previous betrayal. As I look back at it now, I can see I was being tormented by the memories of the past wound that distorted my perception of the present reality. I became defensive and self-protective. My decisions and reactions as a leader were affected. My relationships suffered. I didn't share my struggle with anyone, not even my wife. That should have been a clue to me because Toni and I have always been very open with each other.

As I mentioned in Chapter One, it took a sabbatical, my friend James, a three-day personal retreat and a book on forgiveness to set me free. In a borrowed lake house in Alabama I realized I had not forgiven this man. I vividly remember my conversation with God. During a time of personal confession, God revealed wounds deep in my heart. This was one of those bittersweet times with the Lord. Bitter because God showed me the ugliness of my flesh. Sweet because He showed me the beauty of His grace. Then my Heavenly Father reminded me of a letter I wrote to the man who had hurt me. My tortured mind rationalized the letter as being conciliatory and magnanimous, but in reality it was accusatory and vengeful. I didn't like what I heard God tell me, but I knew He was right. I had not truly forgiven him from my heart. I heard God ask me a few questions: "Is this man's sin against you any worse than what I have forgiven you for? If I forgave you, who are you not to forgive him? How can you praise Me for all the good I worked in you through the situation and at the same time, blame him for it?" With my heart broken, I stood rebuked—I had to forgive him.

> **Unforgiveness is a sign we have devalued God's forgiveness of us.**

As I confessed my sin of unforgiveness to God and forgave the man who hurt me, my heart was transformed. Free! It was like a dam had broken and peace flooded the whole house. I began to sing worship songs at the top of my lungs as the heart once filled with torment was now filled with praise. God reminded me that I had to ask this man's forgiveness for the judgmental letter. While that was one of the most difficult confessions I have ever had to make, it was also one of the most freeing. I am now at peace with all of it. By my estimation, I lost at least a year of peace to the tormentors because of my sin of unforgiveness. What a waste.

### PHIL'S STORY

What Jesus *is* saying in Matthew 18 is that unforgiveness is a sin God takes more seriously than perhaps any other sin. He withholds His protection from us when we refuse to forgive. Why? Because unforgiveness is a sign we have devalued God's forgiveness of us, and it reveals our hearts are not grateful. In essence, our refusal to forgive others dishonors the price Jesus paid for our salvation. As a consequence, God withholds the liberating affect of His salvation in our daily lives. This consequence works out in a particularly strange way when the person we choose not to forgive is ourselves. When we view the things we have done or the offenses we have caused as unforgivable, God disciplines us for that attitude toward ourselves. This can cause tremendous and unnecessary pain. My friend Phil knows this all too well.

## The blood of Jesus cleanses all sin, including the ones committed against me.

I first met Phil a few months ago when He attended a conference our church hosted, which led to Phil visiting our church on Sundays. I called and asked him to lunch, and he accepted. I knew of Phil because he had been a pastor in our area a few years back, but we had never met. Sitting across from him in a booth at Chick-fil-A™, I asked him to share his story with me. Phil was well respected as the founding pastor of a church in our community. A few years ago his daughter was tragically killed in an automobile accident. As you can imagine, the family was devastated. While Phil shared how difficult it was for him and his wife to cope, I tried to imagine how I would handle life if my own daughter had been taken. My heart broke for him.

A mentor once told me that grief and loss will either push a couple together or drive them apart. Unfortunately for Phil and his wife, as they grieved the loss of their daughter, a wedge developed between them, creating a different kind of loss. The wounds compounded as relational mistakes were made. In the end, Phil lost his marriage and his pastoral position. Alone and defeated, he launched into a new career and became a spiritual nomad. As he told me his story, the torment and anguish was clearly evident in his eyes. I quickly recognized the signs of unforgiveness. It was clear Phil struggled with unforgiveness. The most tragic part of his story? The person Phil had not forgiven was himself.

One of the reasons unforgiveness is so offensive to God is this: the Father is satisfied with Jesus' payment for sin, and He thinks we should be satisfied as well. *The blood of Jesus cleanses all sin, including the ones committed against me.* So often the greatest sins against us are those committed by us. Sometimes these are the most difficult to forgive. I asked Phil if he believed God had forgiven him for the things he had done wrong. He looked down at the Styrofoam cup in his hand and quietly said "I've confessed it and yes, God has forgiven me."

"How?" I asked.

He looked at me with a confused look. "Through Jesus' death on the cross."

"That's right." I replied. "Is God satisfied with Jesus' payment for your sin?"

"Absolutely!" he exclaimed. "That's the point of the Gospel."

Then I asked him the big question. "Then why aren't you?"

"Why aren't I what?"

"If God is satisfied with Jesus' payment for your sins, why aren't you?"

"Is this a trick question?" he asked.

"No, it's not. You need to answer the question." I insisted.

At that moment a light went on in Phil's head. I explained to Phil that since God had forgiven him long ago, he was not only holding himself to a higher standard than God was holding him to, but also he was paying a price for a debt that no longer existed.

You see, when we do not forgive (either ourselves or someone else), we are saying that Jesus' death may satisfy God, but it doesn't satisfy us. When we do this, God withholds His protection of us from the tormentors. It is important to remember that torment is not God's preference—freedom is. He allows the torment to serve as a reminder—a symptom—that something is deeply wrong and needs to be addressed. The issue that needs to be addressed is we do not value the blood of Jesus as highly as the Father does. That is unacceptable to God. That's why He allows the torment.

I wish you could have seen what I witnessed next as Phil confessed his sin of unforgiveness and forgave himself. What I saw is something that I've come to expect, but I'm always amazed when it happens. Phil's entire countenance completely changed. It was remarkable. I watched as peace settled over him and a broad smile erupted on his face. The instant he forgave himself, his tormenters left. I asked him, "How's your heart right now?"

He responded, "It feels good. It's calm. It's settled—my heart is settled." When we grabbed lunch together a couple of weeks later, I asked Phil how he was doing. He said, "I cannot remember when I have been more at peace. It has been amazing!"

Father God in Heaven loves us so very much that He sent Jesus to pay for the damage our sin caused to our relationship with Him. Father God is satisfied with the payment Jesus paid. We, who have been forgiven so much, should be satisfied too. Anything less than forgiveness on our part would show the same incredible arrogance and ingratitude the servant in Matthew 18 showed. Arrogance because it shows we have set up a standard higher than God's. Ingratitude because, although we have been forgiven so great an amount, we refuse to forgive so small an amount.

You may be thinking, "Bruce, you don't understand. What happened to me was *huge*." That's what I thought when I heard Sarah describe her story discussed in Chapter One. But at the end of the day, even Sarah agreed our sins against God are far greater than anyone's sins against us. I'm finding when people focus on all the things God has forgiven them for, it becomes much easier for them to forgive others.

### REASONS TO JOIN US

There are three core reasons why we should become active participants in the *Forgiveness Revolution*. First, we owe it to God. He forgave us a debt way beyond our ability to pay. Any debt owed to us is minuscule in comparison. We honor Him by *Forgiving Forward*. Second we find peace and relief from the torment that accompanies unforgiveness. In the parable, the torment ended when the debt was paid. Our debt is considered paid when we forgive our brother from our hearts. Third, we validate the reality of the Gospel in our lives so that others can find the forgiveness God has for them. We will look at this further in Chapter Three.

God expects forgiven people to forgive others. And while He does withhold His protection from us when we don't forgive, He also unleashes His protection when we do forgive.

I cannot describe the joy we experienced as we watched Emma transformed from torment to peace before our very eyes. Now Emma is *Forgiving Forward* by helping others find peace and freedom from torment. She teaches others how to forgive. In fact, not long after that transforming conversation in our living room, Emma went on a mission trip to England to work in a holiday club for children ages 5 to 11. To her surprise, her greatest impact was with adults.

In the first part of her journey Emma encountered a 20-year-old actor and his mother. In conversing with them she recognized they both suffered from bitterness. It was obvious. Emma knew she was on assignment when she heard the mother share a story very similar to what she had just experienced. Her sensitive heart and willingness to share her recent story of forgiveness opened their hearts to find freedom through forgiveness as well.

Emma was also able to recognize the signs of unforgiveness in a young lady who had been abused by her father. After helping her forgive her father, Emma was amazed at the peace and joy in her eyes. In fact, others who knew this girl commented on her countenance transformation as well.

Perhaps what most encouraged Emma was her encounter with an 18-year-old young man whose parents were going through a divorce. She coached him through the process of forgiving his parents and because of the impact forgiveness made in his life, he became an active participant in the Forgiveness Revolution. Emma receives regular reports of this young man *Forgiving Forward* as he helps others forgive.

So how about you? What's your preference today, peace or anguish? To forgive or not to forgive? It's your choice. Personally, I have tried it both ways. I recommend peace—it's just a choice away.

CHAPTER THREE

# Forgiven People Forgive Others
▸▸

**S**uccessful revolutions are inspired by revolutionary leaders driven by a revolutionary cause that people rally around. Revolutionary messages are, at their core, always about freedom.

When Patrick Henry delivered a stirring speech to a crowded court at St. John's Church in Richmond, Virginia, his fiery address is credited for changing the tide. His message convinced the Virginia House of Burgesses to pass a resolution delivering Virginia troops to the American Revolutionary War cause. Upon hearing Henry's charge, those in attendance shouted, "To arms! To arms!" Among the delegates to the convention were Thomas Jefferson and George Washington. Combining the passion of Henry, the literary acumen of Jefferson and the military leadership of Washington, the American Revolution unleashed its fervor and eventually won. This united team came together because they had a common enemy, King George, and a common cause, freedom from over-taxation and tyranny. "Give me Liberty, or give me Death!" became the rallying cry that bonded the colonies together in purpose and passion against England.

## THE CORE MESSAGE OF THE GOSPEL

The same cause is at the heart of The Forgiveness Revolution. This revolution is, at its core, about

**If you cut the Gospel anywhere, it bleeds forgiveness.**

freedom. Yet, the rallying cry is radically different than others. Most revolutions call for a concerted action and attack against an oppressive enemy. The mindset there is to make the rival pay for their oppression. The rallying cry of this revolution, however, is "Freedom through Forgiveness." Freedom from the torture of bitterness only comes through forgiveness. Forgivers let people off the hook rather than desiring to make them pay. This freedom is found at the core of the Gospel message.

If you cut the Gospel anywhere, it bleeds forgiveness. That's why Jesus came to earth. Going all the way back to the Garden of Eden, when God created Adam and Eve, He wanted to cultivate an intimate relationship with them. I can't fully fathom that. God gave them everything they could possible need or even want. He met with them in the morning and in the evenings for walks through the garden and was available for them at their beck and call. The Creator God savored connecting with and doting on His creation. Talk about a charmed life. Adam and Eve had it made. Everything provided. They didn't ever have to worry about right from wrong. Just do whatever God said, and "It's all good." Only one limitation. "Do not eat from the tree of the knowledge of good and evil," (i.e. the knowledge of right and wrong). God had one rule: trust Me in everything, nothing more, nothing less, and everything will be perfect—literally. The ban from the tree was a trust test.

But Adam and Eve failed the test. They did the one thing prohibited to them. Incredible. And when they willfully rebelled against God, they learned the hard lessons of debt as well as cause and effect. They violated God and, by doing so, created a sin debt with no hope of repayment. How does someone recapture perfection? Once you drop below 100 percent, how do you return? The toothpaste never all goes back into the tube, does it? To make matters worse, the debt extended to all of their heirs. Sin became our inheritance. Their debt was passed on to us. (Think the national debt and our grandchildren.)

Again, for reasons I don't understand, God refused to give up on mankind. In His rich compassion, God sent His Son, Jesus, to pay man's sin debt. Perfection required perfection. So Jesus came, lived a perfect life, and by dying on the cross, paid the price only He could pay. Jesus' resurrection proved that the Father, satisfied with His son's sacrifice, forgave the debt. Forgiveness of sins is the very reason Jesus came. (It is interesting to note that God wanted to forgive us a lot more than we *wanted* to be forgiven. It's important to keep this in mind as we process what we are learning about forgiveness.)

After His resurrection, Jesus had a conversation with His disciples that is recorded in Luke 24:46-49. As He gave the disciples their final marching orders, He summarized the Good News for them. *"Thus it is written, that Christ would suffer and rise again from the dead on the third day, and that repentance for forgiveness of sins would be proclaimed in His name to all the nations, beginning in Jerusalem..."* Notice Jesus did not stop with His death and resurrection as the reason He came. No, the cross and the empty tomb were necessary parts of the greater plan. To Jesus, the message of forgiveness is the intended outcome of the incarnation. He endured the cross and conquered the grave to proclaim forgiveness to the world. This is why we can confidently say forgiveness is at the core of the Gospel message.

Jesus went on tell the disciples they were not yet ready to expand the Forgiveness Revolution. He instructed them to wait for the appearance of the Holy Spirit, which would empower them to proclaim the message of forgiveness. This Gospel was so important God the Father sent God the Holy Spirit to help the disciples spread this good news. That same Spirit equips us today with that same theme. Jesus said, *"You are my witnesses of these things. And behold, I am sending forth the promise of my Father upon you; but you are to stay in the city until you are clothed with power from on high"(Luke 24:48-49).* So, as seen in Acts 2, the disciples obediently gathered together until the Holy Spirit fell upon them and they received the power Jesus promised. Their immediate reaction? Check it out. Peter started preaching. Gotta love the progression here. The Spirit's power was followed by an impassioned proclamation of the message of forgiveness.

Peter connected the Old Testament promise of a Messiah with the life, death and resurrection of Jesus. After his sermon, the crowd realized how their sin separated them from God and asked him, "What are we supposed to do about this?" Peter's answer? *"Repent* (i.e. change how you think,) *and each of you be baptized in the name of Jesus Christ for the forgiveness of your sins; and you will receive the gift of the Holy Spirit" (Acts 2:38).* Peter's sermon explained that reconciliation with God—returning to the relationship Adam and Eve first had with God in the Garden of Eden—requires us to acknowledge our sin and receive forgiveness, courtesy of Jesus' death and resurrection.

As we progress through the New Testament, we find forgiveness is continually proclaimed as a central part of the Gospel message and is connected with the empowerment of the Holy Spirit. Let's look at a few examples:

*'The God of our fathers raised up Jesus, whom you had put to death by hanging Him on a cross. He is the one whom God exalted to His right hand as a Prince and a Savior, to grant repentance to Israel, and forgiveness of sin.' (Acts 5:30-31)*

*'And He ordered us to preach to the people, and solemnly to testify that this is the One who has been appointed by God as Judge of the living and the dead. Of Him all the prophets bear witness that through His name everyone who believes in Him receives forgiveness of sins.' While Peter was still speaking these words, the Holy Spirit fell upon all those who were listening to the message. All the circumcised believers who came with Peter were amazed,*

*because the gift of the Holy Spirit had been poured out on the Gentiles also. (Acts 10:42-45)*

*Therefore let it be known to you, brethren, that through Him forgiveness of sins is proclaimed to you, and through Him everyone who believes is freed from all things, from which you could not be freed through the Law of Moses. (Acts 13:38-39)*

*And I said, 'Who are You, Lord?' And the Lord said, 'I am Jesus whom you are persecuting. But get up and stand on your feet; for this purpose I have appeared to you, to appoint you a minister and a witness not only to the things which you have seen, but also to the things in which I will appear to you; rescuing you from the Jewish people and from the Gentiles, to whom I am sending you, to open their eyes so that they may turn from darkness to light and from the dominion of Satan to God, that they may receive forgiveness of sins and an inheritance among those who have been sanctified by faith in Me.' (Acts 26:15-18)*

*In Him we have redemption through His blood, the forgiveness of our trespasses, according to the riches of His grace which He lavished on us. (Ephesians 1:7-8)*

*For He rescued us from the domain of darkness, and transferred us to the kingdom of His beloved Son, in whom we have redemption, the forgiveness of sins. (Colossians 1:13-14)*

You see, any way you slice it, the Gospel involves forgiveness. You cannot communicate the Good News without communicating the radical price Jesus paid to secure our forgiveness. The rallying cry of the Forgiveness Revolution really is "Freedom through Forgiveness!"

### PASTOR JUAN

Recently, I taught this message to a church in San Salvador, the capital city of El Salvador. The main focus of my teaching that morning was on Matthew 18:21-35 and the concept of torture we discussed in Chapter Two. Since I do not speak Spanish, the ministry we traveled with graciously provided a translator. René was amazing. I am pretty animated and expressive when I speak; it has been speculated that if you tied my hands and feet together I probably couldn't put two sentences together. Needless to say, a good translator can make or break you. Rene' was better than good. He even kept my rhythm. When I leaned forward, he leaned forward. When I raised my hand, he raised his hand. When I lowered my voice, he lowered his voice. The Holy Spirit used us in tandem in a remarkable way.

At the end of my talk, I returned the service to Pastor Juan, who has a great heart for God and a sensitive heart for his people. His wife lost her bout with cancer just six months before our trip. The congregation loved him through this crisis and their respect for him grew immensely as they witnessed his faith and the faith of his children. So when he spoke, the congregation listened... sort of like E.F. Hutton.

As Pastor Juan wrapped up our time together, he told his congregation he believed the Holy Spirit was telling him there were five people with significant unforgiveness issues. I'm not sure where you stand on that type of inspiration, but I've come to the conclusion God can do whatever He chooses to do. In this case, six people responded to Pastor Juan's challenge. Now I was really curious. Whether in English or Spanish, five and six are not the same numbers.

I thought to myself, "What's this about Lord?"

He said, "Just wait, you'll see."

Pastor Juan asked me to lead these people through the steps and the prayer of forgiveness (which we will outline in Chapter Eight.) As I walked these six people through the process, I could almost physically see the chains fall off as peace filled the room. In fact, at the very moment they began declaring their forgiveness for the wounds they'd suffered, a deafening clatter of rain hit the metal roof. It came from out of the blue—as if the Holy Spirit was washing away all the pain and torment. As we said "amen," the rain stopped as suddenly as it had started. Amazing!

Each prayer of forgiveness was a miracle—but the best was yet to come. As the six people returned to their seats, Pastor Juan stopped an older gentleman who "just happened" to be the last one to file out. ("Just happened" is often a code word for "God is up to something!") Positioned at the podium, I watched as Pastor Juan shared the Gospel with this well-weathered man and led him to accept the forgiveness of Jesus and find redemption. He came to a new faith in Christ. Now I understood the numerical discrepancy. Five came to *give* forgiveness and one responded with a need to *receive* forgiveness. It added up just right!

Why do I share this story? It illustrates how forgiveness is inseparably tied to the Gospel. While it is true we best learn to forgive others when we first consider the enormity of God's gift of forgiving all our sin debt, it sometimes works in reverse. The gentleman in El Salvador found forgiveness from God when he chose to forgive someone else. There is supernatural power in the selfless act of forgiveness.

> **We never look more like Jesus than when we forgive—except perhaps when we help others find and give forgiveness.**

Perhaps the most significant reason God takes unforgiveness so seriously is that our witness to the Gospel is compromised when we are not modeling what Jesus did for us. As one second century skeptic said, "If you want me to believe in your Redeemer, you are going to have to look a lot more redeemed." We never look more like Jesus than when we forgive—except perhaps when we help others find and give forgiveness. We're never more of a hindrance to the Gospel message than when we harbor unforgiveness. We can't hide it—people can tell. The fellow slaves and the master in Matthew 18 certainly noticed unforgiveness when they saw it. Even though unforgiveness may incubate secretly in our heart for a while, it will always manifest itself in explosively outward ways. The infection of unforgiveness always produces other symptoms, (which we will discuss further in Chapter Nine.)

### Unforgiveness Infects the Church

Could it be that one of the most substantial reasons for a decline in church attendance is linked to unforgiveness? Think about it. How many churches do you know that were started by a strategic church planting initiative? How many churches started as a result of a church split? It's an interesting observation, isn't it? What are church splits typically a result of? Unforgiveness. When two factions in church choose not to forgive, rather than enjoy the fruit of forgiveness (harmonious fellowship), a splinter church is formed. I know of a town where one particular church has a family tree of at least eight churches, each formed due to unresolved conflict. Unfortunately this town is not an isolated situation. The church of Jesus, the Forgiving One, is known in many communities more for its conflict than its love. The community looks on and says, "The peacemakers are at war again!" This is not the original plan, and damages the cause of Christ.

Church trends show pastors are being forced from their positions in increasing numbers. This means there's an escalation in churches going through crisis and conflict. This is a far cry from, "They will know you are My disciples by your love for one another," isn't it? While there are legitimate reasons for a pastor to leave a church, I believe the majority of the time the conflict that leads to a pastor's departure can be traced to unforgiveness. As I stated earlier, I have been around the church all my life and have witnessed my share of church conflicts. I've come to the conclusion that conflict between the pastor and the leadership and/or congregations can often be traced back to old wounds from previous situations. The people of the church have been wounded by previous pastors, and the current pastor pays for the sins of his predecessor. On the other hand, previous congregations have wounded the pastor, and the current congregation is made to pay for the sins of the previous church. One telltale sign of this is when no specific actionable complaints are made against the other party. Often it's more like, "I don't know what it is, but something is just not right." This reveals that the current issue is not really the issue. Often bitterness clouds emotions and replaces specifics with generalities, which are tough to nail down and almost impossible for the other party to respond to. Unfortunately, the predictable end result is relationships are broken, new wounds are added to old ones and people are left wondering "What happened?"

This has certainly been my experience. In the struggle I referred to in Chapter Two, the torment I suffered due to unforgiveness clouded the way I related in the new situation. Rather than functioning in faith and freedom, I began to function out of fear and self-protection. Everybody suffered. At the same time, I believe there were people in the church who reacted to me based on old wounds from previous pastors they had not forgiven. When two parties are wrestling over ghosts of past hurts, nobody wins. In my case, the conflict went unresolved, damaging the reputation of the Gospel in the community.

A friend of mine, Rob, recently took a pastoral staff position in a church, which has a history of trouble with staff members. A few months later, Rob called to vent with me about the restrictive financial policies of the church. It seems that past staff members abused freedoms in the budget process, and now my friend felt handcuffed because of the "sins" of his predecessors. I understand the importance of wise fiduciary procedures in handling money. However, it is important to ask why each policy is in place. Is this policy based on sound Biblical and logical principles or because someone in the past messed up? In other words, do the policies indicate we believe the best or assume the worst? If the answer is, "assume the worst," there is a good chance that unforgiveness is involved. You cannot function out of faith and fear at the same time. Rob was ultimately forced to leave because the administrator was afraid of being burned again. It didn't have to be that way.

### PHIL'S STORY REVISITED

In Chapter Two, I told you about my friend Phil who had been forced to leave his church because of mistakes he had made in the aftermath of his daughter's death. Many people, if they knew of the details of his story, would say that reconciliation in his case would be out of the question. Conventional wisdom says there are certain things that are unforgivable and unrecoverable. But conventional wisdom often undervalues the power of the cross.

**Conventional wisdom says there are certain things that are unforgivable and unrecoverable. But conventional wisdom often undervalues the power of the cross.**

After Phil found his personal freedom through forgiveness, he began to look for ways to get involved in our church and begin to serve. While he listened to God about his future, he was invited to go hear an old friend in town teaching a conference. Phil's former church hosted the event—would there be tension? It would be the first time in ten years Phil had been in the church building. Phil called me and told me he felt God wanted him to go, but he was very nervous. He asked me to pray for him, which I gladly did.

He seemed uneasy when we met a couple of weeks later for lunch. I asked him how it went visiting his old church. He told me that it was like he had never left. People hugged him and loved on him as a long lost friend. I asked him, "Why the uneasiness?" I still chuckle to myself when I reflect on his answer.

"Bruce, I feel torn. I am so grateful to you for helping me find freedom. I am grateful for your church accepting me, and I want to get involved and help. But I feel a strange and strong pull from God to go back to my old church. They welcomed me with open arms and everyone wants me to come back and be a part of them. They assured me all is forgiven, and I think God wants me to go back."

I literally laughed out loud. "You mean you are being reconciled to the church you planted, the church you were forced to leave, and the new pastor and all the leadership is inviting you back? Am I supposed to get in the way of that? Of course you go back. Yay God!"

He called me a few days later and told me that he has been asked to preach there! That is the power of forgiveness.

Why do I share these things? Because people are visiting churches looking for freedom and answers to life problems, but far too often our internal conflicts are drowning out our outward message of forgiveness. They hear us talking about the Prince of Peace, but are they seeing the evidence of His peace in how we relate to one another? What inquirers really want to know is, "Are we smoking what we're selling?" The question they're asking is, "If forgiveness is such a wonderful thing, why aren't you doing it?" You see, our lack of forgiveness hinders our ability to share the Gospel message.

So why is forgiving so difficult for us? Could it be that we really don't believe the Gospel?

The central message of the Gospel is this: The blood of Jesus Christ covers all sins, *including those committed against me.*

Do we believe that? Really?

We like the fact that Jesus' sacrifice covers all of our own sin. That's one of our favorite parts of the Gospel. But are we just as glad that it covers the guy who slandered us, or abused our family or cheated us? Do we believe that *all* sin is ultimately against God? The main question we must wrestle with, regarding forgiveness, is this: if God is satisfied with Jesus' payment for someone's sin, who are we to not be satisfied as well, even if their sin hurt us deeply? Do we realize how anemic a Gospel we are presenting when we fail to incorporate the deep reality of forgiveness into our lives? Believe me, the times we fail at this do not escape the world's scrutiny. But when we remember the true power of our story lies in displaying Christ's redeeming love as we "forgive those who have sinned against us," when we get it right, the watching world is often the first to notice.

## THE WORLD IS WATCHING

On March 2, 2006, a man named Charles Carl Roberts backed a pickup truck to the front of the West Nickel Mines School, an Amish one-room schoolhouse in Bart Township of Lancaster County, Pennsylvania. Roberts entered the schoolhouse at approximately 10:25 a.m. and took the students hostage. Soon, he released everyone except for ten young girls, whom he subsequently shot before turning the gun on himself. Three of the girls died at the scene, two more died early the next morning, and five were left in critical condition at various hospitals. The victims' ages ranged from 6 to 13. The news of this event quickly spread to the national news media. As horrific as the execution-style mass murder of these innocent little girls was, what happened next may have been more of a shock to the watching world.

The echoes of the gunshots were barely silent when the grieving parents expressed words of forgiveness to the family of the man who killed their children. That very day a grandfather of one of the murdered girls warned young relatives not to hate the killer by saying, "We must not think evil of this man."

Another commented, "He has a mother and a wife and a soul, and now he's standing before a just God." A spokesman for the Roberts family reported that an Amish neighbor comforted them hours after the shooting and extended forgiveness. One Amish man held Roberts' sobbing father in his arms, and comforted him for an hour. The Amish community set up a charitable fund for the Roberts family. Thirty members of the community attended his funeral. Roberts' widow, Marie, wrote an open letter to the Amish neighbors thanking them for their forgiveness, grace and mercy. She wrote, "Your love for our family has helped provide the healing we so desperately need. Gifts you've given have touched our hearts in a way no words can describe. Your compassion has reached beyond our family, beyond our community, and is changing our world, and for this we sincerely thank you."

Sadly, many criticized the Amish for forgiving so quickly. Critics expressed the belief that forgiveness should not be granted in the absence of remorse. However, such criticism did not affect the Amish community of Lancaster, Pennsylvania. They were able to forgive immediately because they understood a higher purpose. The Amish community is comprised of men and women of great faith in the providence and sovereignty of God. Their faith enables them to move forward in a crisis, even as horrific and senseless as the murders of innocent schoolgirls, by letting everything rest in the hand of God. While the pain of death is as deep for the Amish parents as it is would be for any of us, they found peace through their understanding of the sovereign grace of God. In an article in the winter 2007 issue of *Willow* magazine, Donald D. Kraybill said this about the Amish ability to forgive:

> *Their model is a suffering Jesus, who carried His cross without complaint, and who, hanging on the cross, extended forgiveness to His tormentors: 'Father, forgive them for they know not what they do.' Beyond His example, the Amish try to practice Jesus' admonitions to turn the other cheek, to love one's enemies, to forgive 70 times 7 and to leave vengeance to the Lord.*

> *Retaliation and revenge are not part of their vocabulary.*

> *As pragmatic as they are about other things, the Amish do not ask if forgiveness works; they simply seek to practice it as the Jesus way of responding to adversaries, even enemies.*

> *Forgiveness is woven into the fabric of Amish faith and that is why words of forgiveness were sent to the killer's family before the blood had dried on the schoolhouse floor. It was just a natural thing to do... the Amish way of doing things.*

> *Such courage to forgive has jolted the watching world as much as the killing itself. The transforming power of forgiveness may be one redeeming thing that flows from the blood that was shed in Nickel Mines.*[4]

It does make a difference whether or not we forgive. It reveals whether or not we believe the message we proclaim. It also exposes our attitude toward God. Earlier we said Jesus did not come just to die and be raised from the dead in order to impress everyone. Instead, He came to provide for the forgiveness of sins. Yet even this wasn't the final objective. The final objective of this redemption story is the glory of the Heavenly Father. When Satan enticed Adam and Eve to disobey God by eating from the forbidden tree, it robbed the Father of glory. He was also robbed of the very thing for which He created mankind—an intimate relationship with each of us. The ultimate goal of the redemption process was to glorify the Father by returning to Him that which was rightfully His. Philippians 2:5-11 confirms this.

*Have this attitude in yourselves which was also in Christ Jesus, who, although He existed in the form of God, did not regard equality with God a thing to be grasped, but emptied Himself, taking the form of a bond-servant, and being made in the likeness of men. Being found in appearance as a man, He humbled Himself by becoming obedient to the point of death, even death on a cross. For this reason also, God highly exalted Him, and bestowed on Him the name which is above every name, so that at the name of Jesus EVERY KNEE WILL BOW, of those who are in heaven and on earth and under the earth, and that every tongue will confess that Jesus Christ is Lord, to the glory of God the Father.*

Everything Jesus did was for the honor and glory of the Father. Everything! Read through the Gospel of John and you'll find that Jesus repeatedly said He came to glorify and do the will of the

Father. His life was all about the glory of the Father, including His death and resurrection.

The Gospel is simply this: Jesus came to glorify the Father by paying the price required to forgive our sins and reconcile us to the Father. When Jesus said, "It is finished," He declared that His work of glorifying the Father was complete. Man's sin debt was covered by His blood. Through the resurrection, the Heavenly Father declared He was satisfied with Jesus' death as payment, and He granted forgiveness. In other words, the glorified Father glorified His Son by accepting the blood of His Son as covering for all sin.

So what about you? Are you willing to be satisfied with the same payment that satisfies God? Are you willing to have the same attitude Jesus possessed? Are you willing to forgive others so the Father is glorified? I hope so, for your sake and for the sake of the Gospel. And if you are, warm up your voice and let loose the revolutionary cry, "Freedom through Forgiveness!

PART TWO

# Forgiving Forward:
# The Model

▶▶

CHAPTER FOUR

# Jesus Predetermined to Forgive
▸▸

With little working capital, Jesse, a highly successful entre-preneur, launched a global communications company based in the Washington D.C. area. Jesse ignored proven business models in selecting his team. Rather than hiring individuals ranked at the top of their class or who had the most potential in the field of communications, he handpicked a "rag tag" group of guys with virtually no prior training. To everyone's surprise but Jesse's, the business exploded, much to the consternation of his competitors.

As the company approached its third anniversary, Jesse planned a much deserved staff appreciation lunch to affirm his team for their dedication and hard work. In such a short amount of time, the skill and proficiency of this group of men had risen to a level above the industry standard. They advanced farther than anyone would've imagined. So Jesse decided to throw a party. He sent an e-mail announcing the mandatory celebration on Thursday at noon. With phone calls forwarded to an answering service and all work ordered to cease, everyone would be available to enjoy the celebration together. There would be food, recognition of achievements, and vision-casting for the future as they celebrated the success of the company.

On Wednesday night before the big event, Jesse worked late. As usual he was the last one to leave the office. In the process of wrapping up after a long day, he checked his e-mail one last time before heading home and noticed an e-mail from his CFO, Judd. Because of Judd's prior experience and training, Jesse had put him in charge of accounting and handling the company books. Judd knew the company inside and out and was perhaps the most qualified member of the team. He knew where the greatest strengths were and the secrets that made their company successful. Jesse was shocked to discover the e-mail wasn't intended for him. Judd had accidentally copied Jesse on the e-mail he sent to their number one competitor. In the e-mail, Judd confirmed a meeting with the president of their chief rival to take place at 1:15 p.m. the next day, the day of the party. He also agreed to accept the compensation offered for turning over the sensitive company documents that could be used to slander and destroy Jesse and his thriving business. Jesse had done nothing illegal, but this inside information could be manipulated and twisted to slander him, giving the appearance of wrongdoing. And, because this rival was politically connected, Jesse could go to jail.

Jesse was stunned by the betrayal of his close associate. What caused him to do such a thing? After all, he had given Judd his first break. Jesse supported Judd during some tough times in his life and thought they had a good relationship. Now what was he going to do?

Several options ran through Jesse's mind. The first thing he considered was having security meet Judd at the door with all of his belongings and escort him back to his car. A second option was saying nothing when Judd arrived at the office. Then, at just the right moment in the middle of the luncheon, embarrass him in front of all his friends and coworkers by exposing the sordid details of his betrayal. He could then arrange to have the Sheriff escort Judd out of the building. Most people would be quick to choose one of these two options. But Jesse wasn't like most people.

Jesse chose a third option. He said nothing to Judd about the
e-mail when he arrived at the luncheon the next day. On the contrary, he greeted him with a hug and honored Judd by escorting
him to his seat. He told him to relax and enjoy himself. He brought
him something to drink. Then at 1:00 p.m., Jesse whispered in
Judd's ear, "I know you have a meeting to go to. Go now, and
I'll cover for you." When Judd left, everyone thought he had left
on an assignment from the boss. Jesse knew full well what his
accountant's betrayal would cost him and his company, yet he still
let him go.

Would you have reacted the way
Jesse did? If you knew someone was
going to betray you ahead of time, how
would you respond? Would you be so
forgiving that you cover for them in the
process of the betrayal? That's exactly
what Jesus (Jesse) did that Passover
night in Jerusalem. He washed Judas'
(Judd's) feet. Jesus called him friend
when Judas led the soldiers to the
Garden of Gethsemane to arrest Him.

**Jesus trusted His Father enough to be able to forgive long before Judas betrayed Him.**

How would you have related to Judas if you knew ahead of time
the brutality you would suffer because of his betrayal? Would you
forgive like Jesus forgave? Would you choose to pre-forgive?

The message of this book is forgiveness. We call it *Forgiving
Forward: Unleashing the Forgiveness Revolution* because we
want people to learn not only how to forgive, but also how to help
other people forgive. But this is not the only implication in the title.
*Forgiving Forward* also implies forgiving in advance. Granted, Jesus
understood that the purpose of Heaven required Judas' betrayal of
Him. There are not many circumstances where the right thing to do
would be to—that God would ask us to—aid someone's sin against
us. But make no mistake, Jesus trusted His Father enough to be able
to forgive long before Judas betrayed Him. That's part of the radical
nature of *The Forgiveness Revolution*. That's the way Jesus forgave.

### OUR MODEL TO FOLLOW

Earlier we said God expects forgiven people to forgive others. It is not an option. We learned in Chapter Two, according to Matthew 18, that God the Father is very serious about the sin of unforgiveness. So it's important that we forgive and that we do it right, which leads us to ask, "How do we forgive?"

The good news is God gives us a model to follow. The model is Jesus. Paul tells us:

> *Let no unwholesome word proceed from your mouth, but only such a word as is good for edification according- ing to the need of the moment, so that it will give grace to those who hear. Do not grieve the Holy Spirit of God, by whom you were sealed for the day of redemp- tion. Let all bitterness and wrath and anger and clamor and slander be put away from you, along with all malice. Be kind to one another, tender-hearted, forgiving each other, just as God in Christ also has forgiven you." (Ephesians 4:29-32)*

In other words, when we speak, our words are to bring life, not death. We are to build people up, not tear them down. Paul goes on to say, "Do not grieve the Holy Spirit." We grieve the Holy Spirit when we speak harsh words to one another and when we don't forgive, when we live in bitterness and malice. Malice wants to make them pay. Malice desires vengeance. But instead we are to *"be kind to one another, tender-hearted* (not hard-hearted), *forgiving each other, just as God in Christ also has forgiven you."*

**Jesus never let the offense determine whether or not He would forgive someone.**

One core element of how Jesus forgave is this: *Jesus never let the offense determine whether or not He would forgive someone.* He was able to separate the person from their sin. He was much more concerned about the person than their actions. It's been said that Jesus loves the sinner but hates the sin. We, however, tend to focus on the actions and rank the offenses to determine whether or not we will forgive. We say, "I could never forgive him for that," or "She's gone too far this time, what she did is unforgiveable." But that's not how Jesus forgives. The person—and their freedom—is much more important than the offense is to Him. Jesus' concept of forgiveness is relational. We forgive people for sins so that relationships can be restored. For most of us, this requires a radical change in the way we think. But once we grasp this truth our ability to forgive will be revolutionized.

The Bible makes it clear that Jesus went to extreme measures to provide for our forgiveness. There are three overarching principles that summarize the uniqueness of the way Jesus forgave. In the next three chapters we're going to examine these three radical ways in which Jesus forgave. In this chapter we'll unpack the principle: *Jesus pre-determined that He would forgive.* Chapter Five shows how *Jesus purposely chose to pay the debt.* Then, in Chapter 6 we'll see how *Jesus left the reconciliation decision up to us.* It is important to recognize that these are very difficult principles to wrestle with. They're not easy. They are simple, but not easy. In many ways they are counter-intuitive to us. But isn't that the way it is with God's truth? God's ways are not our ways. His thoughts are higher than our thoughts, yet, when we understand and apply these new paradigms, miraculous transformations will take place.

### AMANDA'S STORY

One misconception I often hear regarding forgiveness is that "it takes a long time to forgive." The phrase, "forgiveness is a process" is a common belief not only among secular counselors, but also among Christian counselors. The thought process goes something like this: the deeper the wound, the longer it takes to recover. Minor offenses can be forgiven quickly, but major offenses can take years to process and to forgive. I've even heard certain offenses described as "unforgivable." But is this true? Is the speed of forgiveness determined by the depth of the wound? Are there certain offenses that are "unforgivable?"

Not long ago, a friend asked Toni if she would spend some time with fifteen-year-old Amanda. Upon meeting her Toni could not help but notice how emotionless Amanda's eyes were. As Toni listened to her story, she understood why. A few months earlier, an extended family member had brutally beaten and raped her. Clearly distressed Amanda said, "My family has been trying to love me through all this, but I can't receive their love or give any love. I'm just dark inside. I feel dead." Yet, after just 20 minutes of working through God's Protocols of Forgiveness, Amanda chose to forgive her perpetrator and several other people God brought to her mind. She validated her forgiveness by praying a blessing on everyone she had just forgiven, including her attacker. What happened next was miraculous.

**Forgiveness is a decision, not a process.**

Amanda's once dark eyes were now full of joy. "My heart is light. I feel like a new person. I can't believe how good I feel. I can't wait to go tell my mom." When Toni introduced her to me I would never have known she had been wounded. She was immediately set free even though she had experienced one of the worst things a 15-year-old young lady could go through.

Forgiveness is a decision, not a process. When we view forgiveness as a process, we link it to the offense. When we link forgiveness to the offense we place ourselves in the position of having to rank offenses, which requires our focus to remain on the offense. However when we view forgiveness as a decision, we move the focus off of the offense, and it loses its power over us.

Amanda discovered this hidden key of forgiveness. She found that the more decisive she was in her forgiveness, the quicker she found freedom. That's because the quicker we forgive, the more we are forgiving like Jesus. You see, Jesus forgave ahead of time. He chose to pre-forgive. Jesus forgave us before we sinned against Him. He didn't wait until we repented or even until we committed a sin. He chose to forgive us before we were born.

## PRE-FORGIVENESS

One of my favorite sentences in the Bible is found in Ephesians 1:3-14. (That's right, I said sentence. In the original Greek Paul wrote the ultimate run-on sentence.) In this text, Paul answers the question for us as to when God chose to forgive. Let's look at it.

*Blessed be the God and Father of our Lord Jesus Christ, who has blessed us with every spiritual blessing in the heavenly places in Christ, just as He chose us in Him before the foundation of the world, that we would be holy and blameless before Him. In love He predestined us to adoption as sons through Jesus Christ to Himself, according to the kind intention of His will, to the praise of the glory of His grace, which He freely bestowed on us in the Beloved. In Him we have redemption through His blood, the forgiveness of our trespasses, according to the riches of His grace, which He lavished on us. In all wisdom and insight He made known to us the mystery of His will, according to His kind intention which He purposed in Him with a view to an administration suitable to the fullness of the times, that is, the summing up of all things in Christ, things in the heavens and things on the earth. In Him also we have obtained an inheritance, having been predestined according to His purpose who works all things after the counsel of His will, to the end that we who were the first to hope in Christ would be to the praise of His glory. In Him, you also, after listening to the message of truth, the Gospel of your salvation -having also believed, you were sealed in Him with the Holy Spirit of promise, who is given as a pledge of our inheritance, with a view to the redemption of God's own possession, to the praise of His glory. (Ephesians 1:3-14)*

When did God choose to forgive us? He chose to forgive us before the foundation of the world. Before the world was created, before there was matter, time or space, God knew we would sin, and He made the decision, at that time, to forgive us and make us holy and blameless. He pre-determined that He wanted to adopt us simply out of *"the kind intention of*

## His love for us is

*His will."* It was His intention to bring us into a relationship with Him. Not

## greater than His

ours. It was His idea, not a response to a decision of ours. He made the decision

## hatred for our sin.

long before we were capable of making a request. It was His desire to forgive us and restore us to Himself for His own glory. Notice that everything in this passage was all His choice, His intention, His decision for His glory, by His grace.

God, before the foundation of the world, before He created anything, knew what you and I were going to do. He knew every sin we would ever commit and everything we'd ever do to violate His holiness. He knew about it all. And even though He knew everything ahead of time, He declared, "I choose to pay for that. I will redeem it. I will forgive all of it and I will actively work to do whatever is required to make it possible for them to be restored to Me." Again it's all His choice, His intentions, His grace, His work. He didn't wait for us to sin and then say to Himself "Hmmm? Should I forgive them for that? Not sure that's on the list of forgivable things. It may take some time to process this." No! God's choice was made way ahead of time. His love for us is greater than His hatred for our sin.

This remarkable passage in Paul's letter to the Ephesians is a summary of a conversation in Heaven at the beginning of time. God the Father decided that He wanted to adopt sinful man. He wanted to restore us to the relationship with Him that was broken when man sinned in the Garden of Eden. Yet, there was a problem with the adoption. There was the matter of our sin debt. Someone had to pay the price so we could be forgiven. That's when Jesus said, "Father I will pay the price so You can adopt these children (i.e. us.) I will absorb the cost required for the forgiveness of their debt."

Then the Holy Spirit said, "Hey, I want in on the deal. I will be the adoption attorney. I will draw up the paperwork and write an irrevocable contract guaranteeing the debt has been satisfied and assure the adoption is permanent." All this was done knowing that the key element to our adoption was His forgiveness of our sins—decided long before we breathed our first breath.

The model of forgiveness Jesus left for us to follow involves the mindset of *pre-forgiveness*. He made the decision to forgive us long before we admitted we needed it. He knew what we were going to do. "Judas, go do what you need to do." Later in the garden, "Friend, do what you came to do." Shocking isn't it? I don't know about you, but this is way outside of my emotional grid. I have spent hours trying to wrap my head around this concept. As one of my professors in seminary said, "I don't understand everything I know about this." However, I do know it's true. The evidence is clear that Jesus pre-forgave you and me. As we move on in Ephesians 2 we find further evidence of this.

> *But God, being rich in mercy, because of His great love with which He loved us, even when we were dead in our transgressions, made us alive together with Christ (by grace you have been saved)... (2:4-5)*

Death refers to separation from God, and life refers to connection with God. God's choice to offer forgiveness was made while we were separated from Him. The text continues...

> *and raised us up with Him, and seated us with Him in the heavenly places in Christ Jesus, so that in the ages to come He might show the surpassing riches of His grace in kindness toward us in Christ Jesus. For by grace you have been saved through faith; and that not of yourselves, it is the gift of God; not as a result of works, so that no one may boast. For we are His workmanship, created in Christ Jesus for good works, which God prepared beforehand so that we would walk in them. (2:6-10)*

When were the works prepared for us to walk in? Beforehand. Prepared before what? Before we were reconciled. How could that be? Because God knew that in Jesus, all the preparations and requirements for our forgiveness could be completed so we, through faith in the grace of God, would be reconciled to Him. Sounds like a pre-plan to me. Jesus arrived on the planet with a predisposition toward forgiveness. He was ready to forgive because He'd already made the decision to deliver a prepaid package of forgiveness to anyone who asked for it. He expects no less from us.

**It's so much more freeing to forgive than to carry the offense.**

Several months ago, I had lunch with a couple of friends. During the course of the conversation one of these men, Steve, confessed he had an issue with me. I was completely unaware of the conflict. In this particular case, Steve made a false judgment against me and became bitter about it. He had been confronted in his spirit by the Lord and repented, which means he "changed his mind" about what he was upset about. (We will discuss repentance further in Chapter Six.) My friend confessed his judgment against me and asked if I would forgive him. I said "I don't know. Hmmm, I think I need to process this information just a little while. I'll get back to you." No, that might have been what I would've said in the past. But what I said that day was, "Sure I forgive you. I didn't know I needed to, but it's a done deal." You see, the Lord has been teaching me to live with an attitude that forgives everything that anyone does to me. Don't get me wrong. I still struggle with this from time to time. But I have found that it's so much more freeing to forgive than to carry the offense. Steve confessed, I forgave and along with our other friend, we had a great lunch. He was free, I was free and the waitress got a great tip.

### MIKE AND JONATHAN'S STORY

Mike has also learned the power and freedom of pre-forgiveness. Mike's former employee, Jonathan, was a young man who, like many young men, struggled with his faith and had "played the game" spiritually for a long time. He looked good when he needed to, but covered up a lot of junk he was secretly involved in. Earlier, through a series of extraordinary events, the Lord touched this young man's heart, and he had a transformational encounter with Christ. The change was remarkable. Later Jonathan came to me and said, "I have a problem, and I don't know what to do about it. Can you help me?" He then recounted to me that while he worked for Mike at a previous job, he violated the company and got away with it. Completely. He was no longer working for them, and the reason he wasn't still employed by them had nothing to do with his offense. They didn't know what he had done, and there was no way they'd find out on their own. But Jonathan knew and the Lord knew.

"So, what do you think you ought to do?" I asked him.

"I need to make it right. I need to tell my former boss what I did. I need to ask his forgiveness and I need to make restitution for my wrong," he said.

"How much will it cost for this restitution?" I asked. He gave me a figure. "Do you have the money?"

"I have just enough, and then I'll be cleaned out financially. But I need to make this right," he insisted.

"I agree."

That's not even the best part. The greater part of the story happened later when Jonathan arranged a meeting with Mike, his former boss. When they met, Jonathan confessed his sin, much to the surprise of his former boss. He had no idea—had not suspected a thing. Jonathan gave Mike the restitution money and asked, "Will you forgive me?" What happened next was re-markable and, I believe, made Jesus smile. Mike said, "Jonathan, of course I forgive you. I've made the decision to live my life forgiving everything anyone does to me immediately. So this morning before we met, I had already decided that no matter what you told me today, I would forgive you. You are forgiven." They embraced and were immediately reconciled. Amazing! But wait.

**Jesus is calling us, right now, to make the decision to forgive, not only the offenses of the past, but also the offenses of the future.**

There's more. Jonathan was in the process of relocating to another area of the country to follow his dream. Mike made some phone calls and helped the young man land a much-needed new job. He also paid Jonathan to do some odd jobs around his house till it was time for him to move. By forgiving and blessing Jonathan, Mike displayed the attitude of *pre-forgiveness* which reflects the heart of God. That's exactly the model Jesus left for us to follow.

So, what about you? Are you still a *process-forgiver* or are you ready to become a *pre-forgiver*? Is there a Judas in your life that you're having a hard time forgiving or is there a potential Judas in your life you see coming? Jesus is calling us, right now, to make the decision to forgive, not only the offenses of the past, but also the offenses of the future. This doesn't mean you will not feel pain or the wound will not hurt. Jesus suffered unspeakable pain that He knew was coming; yet He still forgave ahead of time. I know, I know, this is radical stuff. But aren't all revolutions driven by a radical thought and radical decisions modeled by a radical leader?

CHAPTER FIVE
# Jesus Purposely Chose To Pay Our Debt
▸▸

would love to sit down and chat with several people from Biblical days. I have many questions for the characters we read
about in Scripture. As a communicator, I'd like to ask Moses
how he overcame his insecurity and fear of public speaking. Moses transformed from a guy with a stuttering problem into a man
who would speak boldly to Pharaoh, the most powerful man in the
world. He became the spokesman for an entire nation. I'd love to
hear how that all happened from the one who lived it.

As a leader, it would be great to sit down with Nathan the
prophet and ask him what it was like to confront King David
about his adultery and conspiracy to commit murder. How long
did he pace outside the throne room before he worked up enough
courage to talk to the king? How strong was the temptation to
sweep the "indiscretion" under the rug? I'd also be fascinated to
sit down with the Apostle Paul. How was he able to convince the
people he once tried to kill that God now wanted him to be their
leader? How did he find the courage to confront Peter about his
hypocrisy?

As a father, I would enjoy talking to David. I'd ask him how it felt when Absalom rebelled and tried to take his throne. I wonder what advice he would give for sibling rivalry, and if he would say that Solomon was always smart? Yet, the guy I would most enjoy meeting at a Starbucks™ somewhere for a long chat over chai lattes, is the father of the prodigal son from Luke 15. You see, I believe this story is more about the father than the rebellious son. There are so many questions I would ask, if I could just sit and talk to this gracious man.

You remember the story. A wealthy man had two sons. The younger son came to his father and said, "Dad, I want my share of your inheritance. I don't want to wait until you're dead; I want it now. Give it to me and I'll be on my way." One of the questions I'd like to ask this dad is how he handled the blatant disrespect this young man displayed. The son was, in essence, saying, "Father, you are as good as dead to me." That is the ultimate insult a son could give his dad. Every father could relate to the emotions that must have welled up inside the heart of the prodigal's dad. I'd ask him, "What was going on inside you when your son asked for his inheritance early? What were your thoughts and feelings? How long did it take for you to decide to say 'yes'?"

Most fathers' reactions would have been to say, "Not on your life, son. Not only will I not give you the money, I'm going to write you out of my will." But that's not what this father did. He had a heart of love and compassion toward his son. He gave the money and let him go. I would love to know why and how he did that.

The prodigal son took the money and ran. He gathered up everything he owned and disappeared. The father did not see him for several months. In my imaginary coffeehouse interview, I would lean across the table and listen to this father recount his emotions and activities while he waited for his son's return. "Was there a time when you thought, 'What was I thinking?' I can't believe I gave him all that money." Being the inquisitive type, I'd also ask, "How much time did you spend on your front porch looking down the road?" "How did you know he would come home?"

Fast forward to the end of the story. The young man wasted all of his inheritance and found himself eating leftovers from pigs, which was the most debased thing a young Jewish boy could do. When he was at his lowest point, he remembered what a gracious man his father was. He decided to go back to his father's house— not looking to return as a son but merely as a servant. He knew he'd be treated well because of how his father took care of his servants. I'd like to know what it was about this father that made his son feel safe enough to return home.

Over the years, I have interacted with many men who have struggled with father wounds. A recurring theme I hear from these men, whether they are older or younger, is that they feel like they could never measure up to Dad's standards. For many, the last place they would go when they hit rock bottom is home. That's because the last person they want to face after they mess up is their dad.

Think about it. Conventional wisdom says, "If you mess up, you better be ready to pay up." "If you can't do the time, don't do the crime." My suspicion is most of us, if faced with the same situation the gracious father of Luke 15 was faced with, would have stood on the porch and waited for the son come to us. We would listen carefully for the repentant attitude. And let's be honest, most of us would make him work his way back to us by granting his request to be treated as one of the slaves, even if just for a short amount of time. Conventional wisdom would want to make sure he had learned his lesson. *Conventional wisdom rarely takes into account the cross.*

This father was different. I'd love to know what made him run to his son after the boy had hurt him so deeply. You see, that is exactly what he did. The father ran to him, grabbed him, embraced him, brought him back into the house, gave him back his room, new clothes, a ring and threw him a welcome home party. The father gave him everything required to reestablish him as a son. By doing all of this, the father was, in essence, settling the son's debt. Why would he do this? I think if we could ask him that question, he would say the decision to forgive and pay for the restoration of his son was made the day his son left, not the day his son returned. The prodigal's father would tell us that he predetermined he would forgive his son and purposely chose to absorb his son's debt. You see, *the father loved his son more than he valued the debt his son created.*

Rebellion always leaves a debt. Wounds always leave their mark. Whether physical or emotional, hurts inflicted upon us by others can leave scars. Violations create relational liabilities. This was true for the prodigal son's father, and it's just as true today. You've seen it in the stories we have already shared with you. The wound of rejection my Papa felt created a relational disconnect with his two close friends. A man violated Sarah when she was only 3 years old, yet a permanent scar could still be seen 56 years later. Discovering her boyfriend had made a choice to leave her for another man caused Emma deep pain. Phil's rebellion cost him his family. The Amish community would never be the same after the loss of 5 of their daughters. I could go on and on. It's just the way sin works. It has been that way since its intrusion into this world.

### PARADISE LOST

In the Garden of Eden, God provided a perfect life for Adam and Eve. The arrangement that God established with them required devotion and belief in Him, nothing else. Another way to say it would be: man owed God glory as an appropriate response to His provision. Glory and honor were the only things God required of man. Man owed it to God to recognize Him as the God of glory. When man sinned, God was robbed of His position of honor in man's life. In essence man attempted to steal from God something that belongs only to God—His glory. And with that, an eternal debt was established. Man now owed God a debt he could never repay.

**We were created to glorify God.**

In his classic treatise, *The End for Which God Created the World*, Jonathan Edwards establishes the position that God created the world and everything in it, including man, for the express purpose of His own glory. The first question in the Westminster shorter catechism is "What is the chief end of man? The chief end of man is to glorify God and enjoy Him forever." We were created to glorify God. It is our obligation to give the Creator God glory in its highest form. Glory means to credit someone or something the honor and value they deserve. When Adam chose to listen to Eve rather than believe God, God was dishonored. By choosing not to believe God, Adam displayed a "devalued" or "de-gloried" opinion of God. In essence, Adam was saying that God was not good enough to be trusted. At that point he "owed" God glory because of his failure to believe and trust God and His holiness. The debt created at the fall of man meant we were now incapable of fulfilling our ultimate purpose. We owe God the perfect expression of trust, honor and glory, but we were no longer perfect and therefore have "insufficient funds" to satisfy God's righteous requirements. This created a significant dilemma for Heaven. God's ultimate purpose was to receive full glory. Part of the fulfillment of His purpose was that man would contribute to the expression of God's glory. God's justice demanded payment for the debt. God's love and mercy called for reconciliation. But how could an irresolvable debt be resolved? How could the unforgivable debt be forgiven? That's where the conversation of Ephesians 1, which we discussed in the last chapter, comes into play.

Before the foundation of the world, God knew man would sin. He also knew there was nothing man would ever be able to accomplish that could settle the sin debt. The Son of God stepped up and said, "Father, for the praise of Your glory, I will pay the sin debt for mankind so You can be reconciled with them." You see, Jesus purposely chose to pay our debt. It is important to note that Jesus made a clear and conscientious decision before we were born to take the necessary action to settle our debt problem. Several passages in Scripture make this clear.

*For while we were still helpless, at the right time, Christ died for the ungodly. For one will hardly die for a righteous man; though perhaps for the good man someone would dare even to die. But God demonstrates His own love toward us, in that while we were yet sinners, Christ died for us. Much more then, having now been justified by His blood, we shall be saved from the wrath of God through Him. For if while we were enemies we were reconciled to God through the death of His Son, much more, having been reconciled, we shall be saved by His life. (Romans 5:6-8)*

*Now if we have died with Christ, we believe that we shall also live with Him, knowing that Christ, having been raised from the dead, is never to die again; death no longer is master over Him. For the death that He died, He died to sin once for all; but the life that He lives, He lives to God. Even so consider yourselves to be dead to sin, but alive to God in Christ Jesus. (Romans 6:8-11)*

*Have this attitude in yourselves which was also in Christ Jesus, who, although He existed in the form of God, did not regard equality with God a thing to be grasped, but emptied Himself, taking the form of a bond-servant, and being made in the likeness of men. Being found in appearance as a man, He humbled Himself by becoming obedient to the point of death, even death on a cross. (Philippians 2:5-8)*

*But when Christ appeared as a high priest of the good things to come, He entered through the greater and more perfect tabernacle, not made with hands, that is to say, not of this creation; and not through the blood of goats and calves, but through His own blood, He entered the holy place once for all, having obtained eternal redemption. For if the blood of goats and bulls and the ashes of a heifer sprinkling those who have been defiled sanctify for the cleansing of the flesh, how much more will the blood of Christ, who through the eternal Spirit offered Himself without blemish to God, cleanse your conscience from dead works to serve the living God? (Hebrews 9:11-14)*

*By this will (God's) we have been sanctified through the offering of the body of Jesus Christ once for all. Every priest stands daily ministering and offering time after time the same sacrifices, which can never take away sins; but He, having offered one sacrifice for sins for all time, SAT DOWN AT THE RIGHT HAND OF GOD, waiting from that time onward UNTIL HIS ENEMIES BE MADE A FOOTSTOOL FOR HIS FEET. For by one offering He has perfected for all time those who are sanctified. (Hebrews 10:10-14)*

We could list verse after verse showing how Jesus paid for our sins. This truth is woven throughout all of the Scriptures. Why? God's holiness required it. That's the theme of the Bible. God's holiness demanded payment for man's sin, and since man couldn't pay the price, Jesus did.

God's holiness has both a negative aspect and a positive aspect. The positive aspect of God's holiness is that everything God is, thinks, says and does is inherently and eternally good and right. He is the very definition of goodness and righteousness. The negative aspect of God's holiness is that everything God is, thinks, says and does is inherently and eternally free from evil of any kind. He is totally free from anything wrong or bad. In Genesis 1:31 when God examined all He created, He declared everything, including man, was very good. It would have to be. God created it.

### 99.9 PERCENT PURE IS NOT PURE

When Adam chose to trust Eve and the serpent, rather than trusting God, man lost his standing as "good." It's interesting to note the serpent tempted Eve to eat from the forbidden tree so that she can become "like God," which she already was—by design.

Genesis 1:27, says *"And God created man in His own image, in the image of God he created Him; male and female He created them."* Eve was like God from the moment she was crafted out of Adam's side. This seems to be a common tactic of God's enemy. He tempts man to take action to become what God has already declared him to be. The moment Adam and Eve chose not to believe and trust God, they were contaminated by sin and lost their identity as "good." *Their attempt to become "like God" resulted in becoming "unlike God."*

Consequently, the first couple lost the privilege of walking with God and communing with Him. Why? Because God is free from evil of any kind. He cannot associate with evil. He demands 100 percent purity. Anything less than 100 percent is not pure.

**Any evil we commit is ultimately against God, regardless of the impact our sins have on other people.**

Contrary to the old Ivory Soap commercial, 99.9% pure is not pure. Would you be comfortable drinking a glass that is 99.9% pure drinking water and .1% rat poison? Me either. Once contaminated by sin, once he became impure, man could never bridge the gap back to God's holiness. He needed help. That's why Christ came. That's what the cross was all about.

Throughout this book we provide examples of how others have followed the model of Christ in forgiving people of the wounds they have suffered. We do so because we believe forgiveness is a very practical decision each of us can make toward those who hurt us. Ephesians 4:32 and Colossians 3:12-13 instruct us to follow the example of Jesus in the way we forgive others. Purposely choosing to pay the sin debt is the one principle of forgiveness we are incapable of reproducing. Paying the sin debt requires a holy righteous sacrifice. Only Jesus meets the qualification. As we read earlier in Hebrews 9, only Jesus' blood was pure enough to pay for the sins of the world.

And, according to Romans 6:8-10, Christ's sacrifice was a one-time payment that was full and complete. Everything was paid in full at the cross. It was a one-time deal that will never need to be repeated.

So how does this apply to us? If we cannot replicate this, what are we to do? I think the first point of application is to realize that all sin is ultimately against God and not us. Remember what David said, *"For I know my transgressions, and my sin is always before me. Against you, you only, have I sinned and done what is evil in your sight, so that you are proved right when you speak and justified when you judge."* (Psalm 51:3-4 NIV). Psalm 51 recounts David's response to God after Nathan the prophet confronted him about

**To expect more payment is to say something was wrong with Jesus and His blood.**

his sin of adultery with Bathsheba and the subsequent murder of her husband. David said, "My sin is only against you, God." I can imagine Uriah standing in the throne room of Heaven, raising his hand and saying, "What about me? He took my wife and my life. Are You sure he didn't sin against me at least a little?" Any evil we commit is ultimately against God, regardless of the impact our sins have on other people. Why is this true? This is true because any evil we do is, at its root, a declaration of unbelief against God. If David had believed God was enough to meet all of his needs, he would not have taken another man's wife or another man's life. If we can wrap our minds around this truth, it will change how we respond to people's negative actions toward us.

The second point of application is for us to recognize the debt was paid. That may sound simplistic, but it is a very important mindset to maintain. One of the key principles of *Forgiving Forward* is: *The blood of Jesus covers all sins, including the ones committed against me.* This means that Christ has covered the sin debt of all people on the cross. To expect more payment is to devalue the sacrifice of Christ for the sins of the world. To expect more payment is to tell God the Father that your standards are higher than His. To expect more payment is to say something was wrong with Jesus and His blood. The truth is, the payment for any sin against us has nothing to do with us. Since all sin is ultimately against God, all payment for sin is to be made to God. It sounds simple when you put it that way, doesn't it? We sinned—God carried the debt—Jesus paid the debt. Simple, but it can be difficult to functionally believe. But believe we must.

So how do we appropriate this personally? Let me encourage you to do three things. First, believe it. Choose to believe that Jesus' death on the cross covers all sin, including the ones committed against you. Make a decision that since God is satisfied, you will be too. It really is that simple. We just have to believe it. The principle is not complicated. If you owed me money, I would have every right to collect the debt. However, if your older brother came to me and paid the debt in full, I would have no right to approach you to collect the debt. In fact, it would be fraudulent of me to do so. Our older brother Jesus has paid the debt of sin on the cross. Therefore, no one owes us anything. The more you embrace this truth for yourself the easier it is for you to forgive, and the more objective you can be when you're helping someone else forgive.

Second, carry an imaginary "Jesus paid it all" stamp with you everywhere you go. You know, the self-inking kind that never runs out of ink. Keep it with you at all times. Then, anytime anyone does anything to you that causes an injury or leaves a wound, just stamp "Jesus paid it all" across it. Everything is paid in full. You will be amazed how easy it will become to forgive when you maintain this mindset.

Third, take every opportunity possible to help other people understand the extravagant payment Jesus made for the sins of the world. The desire for a debt to be satisfied is normal and appropriate. When you're helping someone forgive don't argue against that. God agrees that sins demand a payment. Help them understand this is why Jesus came. He came to pay the debt. The debt for all sin was satisfied on the cross. This is one of the most difficult things for people to grab hold of when you're coaching them through forgiveness. Yet when they do—wow!—it makes all the difference in the world in their ability to forgive.

It's true—Jesus purposely chose to pay our debt. This is the part of the model of forgiveness given to us by Jesus that we don't replicate—we simply embrace it. Nobody could pay for his or her own sin. That's why Jesus paid it for us. Isn't that great? "Jesus Himself is the propitiation (satisfaction) for our sins; and not for ours only, but also for those of the whole world" (1 John 2:2). Spread the word; forgive someone today. And then, help others to forgive someone in their life. It's the revolutionary thing to do.

CHAPTER SIX

# Jesus Left the Reconciliation Question Up to Us
## ▸▶

Toni opened our front door and greeted Elizabeth. A few days earlier at a speaking engagement, Elizabeth asked Toni to help her work through some forgiveness issues she had toward her dad. Elizabeth carried many deep wounds received from him over several years. Not only did Elizabeth's dad hurt her, but, as is so often the case, he resented her for it. We see this a lot. People will fail and, because of their own shame and insecurities, they blame the one they hurt. Offenders often show contempt for their victims—perhaps because the individual reminds them of their failure. This was certainly true in Elizabeth's case. Her father did not acknowledge his offense and continued to wound her. Clearly he was unrepentant.

Toni listened to Elizabeth's story and was able to walk her through the Protocols of Forgiveness to forgive her dad. When she finished going through the protocols, her heart was free because the tormentors were forced to leave. She experienced the miracle of freedom. This miracle thrills us each time we witness it. The evidence was on her face and in her eyes. She still had a question though. Since her dad was unrepentant, how was she to relate to him?

How forgiveness relates to repentance and reconciliation is a question that has caused a great deal of confusion for many people. I have a pastor friend who believes we are under no obligation to forgive unless the offending party repents. In other words, unless the other person asks for forgiveness, it would be inappropriate to forgive them. Another author defines forgiveness as "a commitment by the offended party to pardon graciously the *repentant* from moral liability and to be reconciled to that person, although not all consequences are necessarily eliminated."[5] According to this definition, forgiveness and reconciliation are the same because it makes our forgiveness dependant on the offender's repentance. The author is saying repentance must precede forgiveness. By this logic, the offending party controls the offended party. If the one who caused the wound refuses to acknowledge their wrong, the wounded party is locked in the state of unforgiveness. As we have seen, God disciplines unforgiveness as harshly as any other sin. If this line of thinking were true, there would be two offenses: the original offense and the offense of holding the injured party hostage to unforgiveness. This would be so unlike God and would certainly be different than the model Jesus left for us to follow.

**Reconciliation between the offended party and the offending party requires both forgiveness and repentance.**

In Chapters Four and Five we discussed how Jesus predetermined He would forgive and purposely chose to pay our debt. The third characteristic of Jesus' model of forgiveness is *He left the reconciliation decision up to us.* Jesus made the decision, and provided the provision for our forgiveness, then He *waited* for us to recognize our need before reconciling with us. He waited for us to repent. Jesus forgave the sins of the whole world—but the whole world is not reconciled to God. Why? Because Jesus never forces anyone to accept His forgiveness. He never forces anyone to be in a reconciled relationship with Him.

God the Father loves us so much He did not want to live without us. This includes everyone. He sent Jesus to pay for our sins so forgiveness of sins could be offered to the whole world. Yes, the offer of forgiveness is to the whole world. *"My little children, I am writing these things to you so that you may not sin. And if anyone sins, we have an Advocate with the Father, Jesus Christ the righteous; and He Himself is the propitiation for our sins; and not for ours only, but also for those of the whole world." (1 John 2:1-2)* Yet not everyone is reconciled to God, even though that is clearly God's desire. Why not? Because everyone hasn't repented. Repentance is the key. Forgiveness is only one side of the coin. The other side of the coin is repentance. *"The Lord is not slow about His promise, as some count slowness, but is patient toward you, not wishing for any to perish but for all to come to repentance." (2 Peter 3:9)* Reconciliation between God and man requires *both* forgiveness *and* repentance. Forgiveness is up to God. Repentance is up to us. Once both take place, *then* reconciliation is possible. The same is true between man and man. Unless there is forgiveness and repentance, reconciliation cannot take place. Reconciliation between the offended party and the offending party requires both forgiveness and repentance. In Elizabeth's case, unless her father recognized and repented of his sin against her, they could not live in a reconciled relationship.

### RECONCILIATION = FORGIVENESS + REPENTANCE

Throughout the years I have heard many sermons dealing with repentance. More times than I can count I have heard repentance defined as "turning around and changing direction." This definition says repentance is a change in behavior. I used to believe this and have even taught this in the past. But that is not what this word means. The Greek word for repentance is *metanoia.* The main word in the compound is *noia,* which means "mind, understanding" in the noun form and in the verbal form "to direct one's mind to; to perceive mentally; to think; to understand; to know."[6] The prefix to the word *metanoia* carries the meaning of "after" or "change." Thus the word means "to perceive or believe after," or "to change your mind." Therefore, repentance means to believe differently, to have reconsidered and changed your mind and reached a different conclusion. It is interesting that in the Biblical world repentance is not just a cognitive issue; it is also an issue of the heart. In the Bible, the heart is the place where thoughts and teachings are believed and owned. *"Pay attention and listen to the sayings of the wise; apply your heart to what I teach" (Proverbs 22:17 NIV).* When Solomon asked for wisdom to govern well, God said, *"I will give you a wise and discerning heart" (1 Kings 3:12 NIV).* True repentance toward God also involves the heart. *"For with the heart a person believes, resulting in righteousness, and with the mouth he confesses, resulting in salvation" (Romans 10:10).* We receive truth in our mind; we believe and embrace it in our heart. This implies that repentance is more than just a mental assent to something—it's a heartfelt belief.

**The behavior is not the focus of repentance; the behavior is the evidence of a changed mind.**

What we believe determines what we do. Beliefs always dictate behavior. In the religious world, success ("spirituality") is so often determined by how well you keep the rules. The focus is on behavioral modification and sin management, usually with a list of regulations and standards given to which everyone must conform. Under this type of system, behavior is driven more often by fear than heart agreement. It has been proven that the behavior of others can be controlled without affecting their hearts. History has demonstrated that given the right external circumstances and pressures, abusive leaders can make others do whatever they wish. When the controlling circumstances and pressures are removed, the new behavior does not continue. Yet if someone's belief system changes, his or her behavior will change—every time. Why? Because the behavior is determined by what we believe. That's why the essence of repentance for people of faith is not "changing my behavior" or "changing my direction" but rather "changing my mind." The behavior is not the focus of repentance; the behavior is the evidence of a changed mind.

Jesus instructed the disciples to proclaim the Gospel of repentance, which would allow people to receive the forgiveness of God. This repentance is choosing to change one's belief about God and about life. It is rethinking or changing the core belief system that says, "I can make my life work on my own, and I really don't need God." The repentance that leads to salvation declares that God is right and we are wrong. We choose to believe God, and we trust Him to make us holy through the death and resurrection of Jesus, so we can have a relationship with Him. We are reconciled when God's forgiveness combines with our repentance. As we've discussed, God's decision to forgive us was already settled before the foundation of the world and the payment was made on the cross. My reconciliation with Him occurred when, as a young boy, I repented of my sin and declared my belief in God and accepted the forgiveness provided to me by Jesus Christ.

Reconciliation is the restoration of estranged parties to a good relationship. In order to restore the relationship between God and man, the factors which caused the enmity must be addressed and removed. Both parties have a responsibility. Theologians refer to God's part as the atonement. Atonement is what Jesus did by paying for our sins on the cross. It is not my intent to resolve the big atonement issues that have been debated by theologians for centuries. I just know that God decided before He created the planet that Jesus would pay the price to atone for man's sin. He made the decision before we were born, before we sinned, and before we repented. I have not found an account in Scripture or throughout history of anyone being turned away from Jesus who came to Him in repentance. He received everybody who confessed their sin and declared their belief in Him as the Son of God, the Savior of the world. The decision to forgive was made by God before we repented. Those who think differently have to wrestle with the question of what did John mean when He said Jesus is the satisfaction for the sins of the whole world. (1 John 2:2) The Biblical record clearly shows forgiveness can, and does occur without reconciliation.

### COME TO THE TABLE FIRST

Let me try to illustrate this. Let's say reconciliation is a high-top table with two chairs. One chair is the chair of forgiveness; the other is the chair of repentance. The table is needed because somebody wounded someone else. The wounded person is standing at a distance on the forgiveness side. The offender is standing at a distance on the repentance side. In order to be seated at the table, the wounded person must present a ticket stamped "forgiveness." The offending party cannot be seated until they present a ticket stamped "repentance." Those two tickets are completely independent of each other. But reconciliation will not take place until both parties are seated.

**We believe forgiveness is a matter of faith and has more to do with our relationship with God than the person who hurt us.**

Either party is free to make the move first. If the wounded party presents his ticket of forgiveness and is seated at the table and the offender is unrepentant, there is no reconciliation. If the offender, on the other hand, presents his ticket of repentance and is seated at the table, but the wounded party is unforgiving, there is no reconciliation. Reconciliation can only take place when both parties bring their respective tickets, forgiveness and repentance, together to the table.

In the case of man's offense against God, Jesus came to the table with forgiveness long before we brought our repentance. He sat at the table of reconciliation waiting patiently for us. In the same way, God often calls the forgiving one to the table before

He calls the repentant. Why is this true? We believe forgiveness is a matter of faith and has more to do with our relationship with God than the person who hurt us. If, when wounded, we wait to be seated at the reconciliation table until after the one who wounded us repents and is seated, then our forgiveness is, in some degree, based on their actions. If we come to the table first, then our forgiveness is based on God's actions—Jesus' death on the cross. Arriving first demonstrates our faith and glorifies God much more than coming to the party last—and believe me, reconciliation is a party!

### Brad and Molly's Story

I answered the phone, and the voice on the other end said, "My name is Brad. A mutual friend gave me your number and suggested I call you. I've done some terrible things and have hurt my wife deeply. We're in a very bad place. My friend thinks you might be able to help, although it looks hopeless to me. Would you be willing to meet?" At the arranged time, we welcomed Brad and Molly into our home. Brad had a beaten puppy look about him, and Molly carried a massive invisible shield of ice, which she kept between her and her husband. As Brad told his story to us, we understood why.

Three weeks earlier Molly discovered Brad's pornography addiction. When she confronted him, he confessed to a 20 to 30 hour per week porn habit. He also confessed to multiple adulterous relationships including prostitutes, Molly's best friend, and Brad's best friend's wife. Molly had not suspected any of this before she caught him looking at porn. Needless to say, she was in shock. She told him she would not divorce him because she didn't want their three daughters to grow up in a divorced home, but she never wanted him to touch her again. "We will stay married for the sake of our kids, but our relationship as husband and wife is over." Both of them were devastated by his sin.

A couple of days after the initial confrontation, Brad picked up his Bible from a shelf in the living room. When he opened the Bible, the first thing he read broke something inside him. He ran out the backdoor of their house, over a hill and sat under a cluster of trees and continued reading. For two hours he read the Bible and for the first time understood the grace of God and the forgiveness provided for him through the blood of the cross. He was dramatically transformed. Heart cleansed. Desires changed. The lust gone.

Molly recognized the change but could not get over the offense. After Brad finished sharing his story, Toni looked at Molly and asked, "How are *you* doing?"

> Tearing up, she said, "I thought we had a great marriage. I had no idea. I swore I would not be like my mom, but now I have become my mom, and he has become my dad."
>
> "What do you mean by that?" we asked her.
>
> "My father used to cheat on my mother and would use me as an alibi. He would take me with him and leave me in the car while he was inside with the other women. One day I went to find him. I looked through the window and saw what he was doing."
>
> It was clear this memory tormented her.
>
> At this point I looked at Brad and asked who hurt him as a child. He looked at Molly, and she looked back at him, and asked, "Did you tell him?"
>
> He replied, "I didn't tell him anything."
>
> They both had a "how did he know that?" look in their faces. I assured them I had not been told anything but that we had a partner—the Holy Spirit—who guides us as we coach others. I asked the question again, "Who hurt you when you were younger?"
>
> "My sister, when I was five," he answered.
>
> "Your sister? How old was your sister?" I inquired.
>
> "She's about 10 years older than me," he responded.
>
> Then cautiously I asked, "What did she do?"

He began to describe the sexual abuse his sister committed against him from the time he was five years old until he was eleven. Horrific abuse. We expressed our grief and outrage over what he endured. We explained how the torment of those wounds was driving his dysfunctional behavior. We helped them both to understand how this would explain the risky, almost incestuous, affairs he had with those so close to him and his wife. We asked if he wanted to be set free from the torment of what happened to him as a child. He said, "Yes."

We gently told him, "You must forgive your sister." He responded by telling us that, although she no longer sexually abused him, she still abused him emotionally. He shared more examples of the wounds. Clearly, his sister was not repentant.

Conventional wisdom wouldn't give this couple good survival odds, but conventional wisdom doesn't understand the power of forgiveness. We began to walk Brad through the protocols of forgiving his sister. As he slipped off the couch and onto his knees, Molly slipped off the other end of the couch as well. They were still separated by our coffee table. As he began to forgive the list of wounds from his sister, Molly began to weep uncontrollably. Toni knelt beside her and cradled Molly in her arms. After Brad finished forgiving the wounds inflicted by his sister, I coached him through the process of forgiving himself. When he finished they both returned to the couch and I asked him, "How is your heart?" He told us he would never have believed his heart could be any better than the day he trusted the Lord, but in fact it was better now than ever. He was unmistakably free.

Molly then said, "I don't understand what just happened. When Brad was forgiving his sister I felt overcome with intense pain and grief over what he endured—almost unbearable to me. But when he forgave himself, I didn't feel the pain any more. I didn't feel anything at all. I don't understand?"

"Is that a good thing or a bad thing?" I asked.

"It's a good thing. I didn't hurt when I heard him pray through the list of women he had affairs with. This is the first time in three weeks I have not felt pain about what he did. Instead, I saw just how much his sister hurt him."

Then Toni piped in, "Molly, I believe that you will not be free, totally free, from the torment you have experienced until you also walk through forgiveness. It is crucial you not only forgive your husband for the wounds he inflicted upon you, but also forgive your father for the wounds he caused." She agreed and began the process of forgiving both Brad and her father. When she finished, the change in her countenance was remarkable. As they stood up to leave, Molly embraced Brad for the longest time. That hug was the first time in over three weeks she had touched him. Not only that, but on the way home she unbuckled her seat belt and slid over on the bench seat and snuggled with him. He told me he almost wrecked the truck when she made the move.

**I can't explain it, but something happens in the supernatural realm toward the offender when we forgive.**

We saw them about a month later, and she told us their marriage has never been this good. The same can be said for the joy of their salvation.

Brad and Molly's marriage was saved through forgiveness. It is important to note that neither Brad's sister nor Molly's dad have shown any evidence of repentance or desire for reconciliation. Yet it is undeniable that these two people have forgiven—ending *their* torment.

Most of the time, we do not recommend the forgiver go to the offender to proclaim their forgiveness. Sometimes that's important, but the majority of the time going to the person who has wronged us hinders reconciliation. It is only when they have come to a point of repentance that reconciliation is possible. We can get in God's way when we get too aggressive in trying to rush the process. However when we forgive and trust God, He begins to work on the offender to bring them to repentance.

This was true for Elizabeth, who we introduced to you at the beginning of this chapter. We connected with her a few weeks after Toni coached her through forgiving her dad. She said to us,

"You'll never guess what happened. Two weeks after we met, I visited my parents and went in to check on Dad. Before I could say anything to him, he told me he was sorry for the things he'd done to me and wanted to know if I could ever forgive him. I told him I had already forgiven him. It was unbelievable! Our relationship has never been this good." It's clear

**Repentant people are always safe with Jesus.**

that after Elizabeth forgave her dad; God worked in her dad. I can't explain it, but something happens in the supernatural realm toward the offender when we forgive.

It's true. Jesus forgives us but leaves the reconciliation question up to us. He offers His forgiveness and He *waits* for us to repent. And isn't it great to know that repentant people are always safe with Him? They *really* are. There is no better example than the thief on the cross. Jesus was crucified between two criminals guilty of capital crimes. One of the thieves mocked Jesus. Yet the other criminal rebuked the first thief by saying, "'*Do you not even fear God, since you are under the same sentence of condemnation? And we indeed are suffering justly, for we are receiving what we deserve for our deeds; but this man has done nothing wrong.' And he was saying 'Jesus remember me when You come into Your kingdom!'*" *(Luke 23:40-42)* This man clearly acknowledged his sin and declared his faith in Jesus as God's Son, the Savior of the world. He repented. What was Jesus' response? *"Truly I say to you, today you will be with Me in Paradise" (Luke 23:43).* It was as if He said, "You're safe with me. Welcome to the Kingdom."

Repentant people are always safe with Jesus. The reason for this is that Jesus separates the person from their sin. He loves us and hates our sin. That's why He forgave ahead of time. He was so concerned about us that He dealt with our sin so He could restore us back to a relationship with the Father. *Jesus never let the offense determine whether or not He would forgive someone.* His love for the Father and for us is what makes repentant people safe with Him.

*The question that remains for us is this, "Are repentant
people as safe with us as they are with Him?"*

People who hurt us should be as safe with us as they are with
Jesus. Our job is not to judge the sincerity of someone's repentance. Our job is to forgive and welcome the repentant one back.
But just like with Jesus, not everyone will repent and desire reconciliation. There are people in our lives who have hurt us deeply,
whom we have forgiven, but they have not changed the way they
think about their offenses. They have not repented for the wounds
they have inflicted upon us. We are not reconciled. Do we desire
reconciliation? Absolutely. In fact, we pray for it all the time. But
the reconciliation is not our decision—it's outside our control.
Amos 3:3 says, *"Can two walk together, unless they are agreed?"*
There is a trust issue when someone is unrepentant. If someone
does not agree what they did was wrong, they are likely to repeat
the offense. Particularly in cases of physical and emotional abuse,
it may not be safe for the wounded person to be alone with the
offender. Forgiving someone does not give them the right to hurt
us again. Jesus did not entrust himself to the Pharisees because
He knew their intentions. (John 2:24-25) Wisdom calls on us to
protect our hearts from further wounds. Yet, through forgiveness,
we do not think the same way about what happened. We now view
what happened through the lens of the cross.

What would we do if the offender came to us and repented?
What if they said, "We are so sorry for what happened. We were
wrong. Will you forgive us?" We would say, "Of course. It's
already been done. We made that decision a long time ago." And
we have. We have committed to God that the automatic answer
to anyone who seeks our forgiveness is—Yes! Because that's the
way Jesus did it. We want repentant people to be safe with us
because they are safe with Him. Are they safe with you? They can
be if you learn to forgive and *wait*. Wait for their repentance—the
last stage necessary for full reconciliation.

# PART THREE

# Forgiving Forward: The Method

▶▶

## CHAPTER SEVEN
# We are Our Brother's Keeper
## ▶▶

answered my cell phone late one evening and heard Susie's distressed voice on the other end saying, "Pastor, I don't know what to do. Roger has checked into a hotel in North Atlanta after visiting his old drug supplier. He told me not to call you, but I'm calling anyway because I just don't know what to do." Roger and Susie had attended our church for a couple of years. They came from very difficult family backgrounds and were both previously divorced. Roger's father abandoned the family early in his life, the first of many personal wounds—several of which were self-inflicted. I had the privilege of helping Roger come to faith in Jesus and baptized him in a lake behind our church. However, because of the many deep wounds of his past, Roger had developed coping mechanisms that automatically kicked in when he faced stress. His old habits took over when he had a rough day or something went wrong. Without thinking, he chose addiction. And that was right where he found himself that night.

I assured Susie we were committed to her and Roger. After praying and encouraging her to stay strong in her faith, I hung up the phone and called Roger. He didn't answer. I knew he had his phone with him because Susie just talked to him. So, I called again. Still no answer. On the third attempt (I was determined) Roger answered and sheepishly said, "hello."

"Roger what are you doing?" I asked.

"I'm okay," he replied.

"That's not what I asked you. What are you doing?"

"Did Susie call you?" he demanded.

"Yes she did. What are you doing in a hotel room in North Atlanta?"

"I don't want talk about it. Leave me alone, Pastor."

"That's not going to happen, Roger."

"I really messed up this time."

"I know, but we're going to help you."

Roger was not altogether happy to be having this conversation, although, to his credit, he didn't hang up. I knew in his current condition any confrontation or conversation we might have that night would be remembered by only one of us the next morning. So, in consultation with James, my counselor friend, and Ed, another leader in the church, I instructed Roger to stay in his hotel room and sleep it off. James had a long conversation with Susie that night and assured her we would deal with this in the morning when Roger was sober.

**We find that most, if not all, addictions and interpersonal conflicts are rooted in unforgiveness.**

At nine o'clock the next morning James, Ed and I arrived at Roger's hotel room with a couple of chicken biscuits and some strong coffee. We were uninvited—but also undeterred. Roger was a friend of ours, and he was in trouble. And the biggest threat to Roger was Roger. We were there to rescue him from himself.

We find that most, if not all, addictions and interpersonal conflicts are rooted in unforgiveness. When a wound is not cleansed
with the antiseptic of forgiveness, the infection of bitterness in-
variably takes over. The process is so subtle and deceptive that
one tends to focus on the wound as the source of the pain when
in reality the pain you're suffering is because of the lack of forgiveness. Addictions address the symptoms, not the cause. People
medicate with sex, drugs, alcohol and other addictions such as
painkillers, rather than treating the infection of bitterness. This
was certainly true of Roger. We saw it long before he was able to
recognize it. Roger needed help.

Though hesitant at first, Roger began to open his heart and
share his story with us. He'd been hurt deeply by so many people,
and he had hurt others as well. As we walked him through the
Protocols of Forgiveness (which we will outline for you in Chapter
Eight) we could visibly see the healing and transformation take
place. For over 45 minutes, the three of us observed Roger forgive
wound after wound including many that were self-inflicted.
When he finished I asked him the question, "How's your heart?"
He answered, "It's calm and light. I feel like I'm a new me. I'm
free." And he was. From that day on he has been drug-free. His
addiction ended when he forgave. In spite of the fact Roger didn't
initially want us there, James, Ed and I witnessed the transformation forgiveness brought to Roger's life.

### OUT OF OUR COMFORT ZONE

We are called to speak into each other's lives. We are account-
able to one another. We are our brother's keeper. As we discussed
in Chapter One, God's answer to Cain's question is opposite of
what most people want it to be. What happens to our brother is our
business. Really? Yes. Does that mean if people are struggling I'm
supposed to help them? Yes. Even if they don't invite me, I still
have an obligation from God to speak into their lives? Yes. Most
of us are not comfortable with this concept. But I think comfort

may be overrated. In fact, significant interpersonal transactions and developments are often uncomfortable. I can look at my own marriage and see the greatest growth times in our relationship were preceded by difficult and uncomfortable interactions.

This is especially true when it comes to unforgiveness. Bitterness has a way of blinding us from the reality of our own sin. You've seen it, haven't you? The person being consumed by bitterness is often the last person to recognize it. A friend of mine once told me, "no one who believes a lie believes that the lie they're believing is a lie." Got that? People believe what they believe, whether or not it is true. It often takes someone intervening to help someone repent (change their mind) and turn from the lie to the truth.

I love Colossians 1:27-28, which is Paul's summary statement of ministry. He sums up the message of Christianity in verse 27 as, *"Christ in you the hope of glory."* The core of the Gospel is Christ is in us, which gives us the assurance of sharing in the glorious Kingdom of God. Paul then describes our responsibility to be a steward of that message when he says, *"We proclaim Him, admonishing every man and teaching every man with all wisdom, so that we may present every man complete in Christ"* (Colossians 1:28). Notice the fourth word, *admonish*. This word means to correct through instruction and warning. There are not many people I know who relish the thought of being admonished. Few of us really enjoy being corrected. But that's what this passage says we are to do for one another. We are to proclaim Christ, who is our hope of glory, and admonish or correct every person with the goal of helping him or her become complete and mature in Christ. It doesn't say to wait for the invitation. It says that we are to admonish and teach. Why? Because people often need help long before they recognize they need help. If we wait for people to ask us to admonish them we will never carry out the command of this passage. That's why my two friends and I went, uninvited, to a hotel room in North Atlanta that morning to help Roger. We didn't go because we had nothing else to do. All three of us had to rearrange our schedules to go there. The reason we went was because Roger was caught in a trap (see Galatians 6:1) and needed our help. Confronting him was part of our responsibility to help him become a little more complete in Christ. But what if he didn't want to hear what we had to say? That wasn't the point. What he needed was more important to God than what he wanted.

We are our brother's keeper. It's part of the assignment we have from God. We see this in 2 Corinthians 5:18-19, *"All these things are from God, who reconciled us to Himself through Christ and gave us the ministry of reconciliation, namely, that God was in Christ reconciling the world to Himself, not counting their trespasses against them, and He has committed to us the word of reconciliation."* We have been assigned the responsibility to go and help people who are far from God. We are to confront them in a gentle and sometimes firm way to help them see the truth of God's love for them so they can turn to Him. This text makes it clear we are to initiate the conversation.

You need more proof? Let's look at Matthew 18:15-17: *"If your brother sins, go and show him his fault in private; if he listens to you, you have won your brother. But if he does not listen to you, take one or two more with you, so that by the mouth of two or three witnesses every fact may be confirmed. If he refuses to listen to them, tell it to the church; and if he refuses to listen even to the church, let him be to you as a Gentile and a tax collector."* In the section right before His discussion about unforgiveness and torment, Jesus tells us that if our brother sins we are to go to him and confront him. What? Go to someone and confront them about their sin? In this culture? Really? We are to point out someone's fault? Yes, that is what the text says.

But what if he does not want you to? You do it anyway. If he listens to you, you've won your brother. If he doesn't listen to you (he's not receptive), you are to find a couple of other people who have seen the same sin in him and can witness the same things to him, and you join together to confront him a second time. Does that mean that if they tell you to leave them alone when you confront them, you don't? Yes, that is what the text says. And if he does not listen to the small group, you take it to the church. What? Isn't that an invasion of their privacy? Obviously God is less concerned with the issue of privacy than we are. We are our brother's keeper.

Why is it so important to God that we intervene in someone's life when they are caught in a sin? The

**Friends don't let friends live in unforgiveness.**

answer is simple. God knows sin is *always* harmful. The greatest act of love is not found in tolerance, but rather through intervention. There is a popular ad campaign against drunk driving that says, "friends don't let friends drive drunk." Why? Because if you let your friend drive drunk, he will be in danger of hurting himself and other people. It's just too dangerous. Friends don't let friends live in unforgiveness for the same reason. It's damaging to them, and it often hurts others as well. True friends do what they can to help others learn to forgive.

### No Judgmentalism Allowed

It's important here to insert a clarification of what I'm not saying. I'm not saying we should go off on a crusade of admonition. We are not to go around like the proverbial bull in the china shop and tell people "forgive or else." In Galatians 6:1, Paul makes it very clear how important it is for us to provide the kind of help we're talking about with the right spirit and motive. Coupled with the instruction to get involved in someone's life who is caught in a sin is the requirement to check our own hearts first. In Galatians 6:1 we read, *"Brethren, even if a man is caught in any trespass, you who are spiritual, restore such a one in a spirit of gentleness; each looking to yourself, so that you too will not be tempted."* Notice the qualification for those who fulfill the privilege of confrontation. The prerequisite is that one be "spiritual." Paul defines what it means to be spiritual in the previous chapter as one who "walks by the Spirit." A person who is walking by the Spirit will confront in a way that is consistent with the Holy Spirit. So Paul says, "You, who are controlled by the Holy Spirit, when you see someone caught in a trespass, are to go to him in a spirit of gentleness." Why gentleness? We are to go in a spirit of gentleness (a fruit of the Spirit) because that's how we would want to be approached. Someone who's controlled by the Holy Spirit recognizes that all ground is level at the foot of the cross, that we're all screw-ups, but God loves us anyway. If I see someone caught up in sin, all I can be sure of is that they are caught today and I am not. **You cannot help others forgive if you are judgmental toward them.** Tomorrow the situation could be reversed, and I could be caught and in need of their help. Any of us, at any time, are susceptible to and capable of committing any sin. That's why we forgive others so quickly, because we need to be forgiven regularly. Paul tells us to look to ourselves so we don't become arrogant when we help someone else.

There is a way to do it right, and we must be careful, but we are to confront. We are to move into someone's life, and we are to help them. There is no room for a judgmental or superior attitude when you're trying to help someone. You cannot help others forgive if you are judgmental toward them. But, with the right spirit, you can deliver a miracle of freedom to a friend or acquaintance. When you do, you'll realize that with this obligation comes great privilege and joy.

### IT IS A PRIVILEGE

The big idea of this chapter is this: *God has given us the privilege of setting people free by helping them forgive.* It is an incredible privilege. Three of the greatest joys I have personally experienced in my life have to do with forgiveness. First, I have experienced the incredible joy of receiving the forgiveness of God when I put my faith in Jesus and His death for me on the cross. Second, I have experienced the joy of being released from torment

112 ▶▶▶                                     *Forgiving Forward: The Method*

by forgiving those who had violated me. Third, I have participated in the process of helping others find deliverance from torment through forgiveness.

Recently, in conjunction with a student campus ministry, we spent time at a university teaching the message of *Forgiving Forward.* I taught at night and Toni and I counseled students during the day. The campus ministry leader posted an appointment sheet and students signed up by the hour to meet with us. One day we started meeting with students at eight o'clock in the morning and didn't get settled back in our room until 1:30 the next morning. We had about an hour break to eat dinner and to freshen up before the night session. Every student we interacted with experienced breakthroughs. It was one of the most exhilarating and exhausting days. The transformations we observed were remarkable and a lot of fun to watch—so blessed that God allowed us to be a part of it all.

It is an amazing privilege to deliver the miracles of forgiveness. It's also an assignment from God. Helping people find freedom through forgiveness is an assignment from God for *all* His children. It takes a sensitive and humble spirit. It takes courage and gentleness. Sometimes people will invite you. Sometimes they'll put their name on a clipboard to schedule to meet with you, and sometimes you need to ask questions to navigate your way into their hearts. That's why we're writing this book, to help you recognize the signs of unforgiveness and to train you in the process of *Forgiving Forward.* I suspect everyone who reads this book knows someone who is bitter but doesn't recognize it. Yet, everyone around them can see it. There are also people who will readily admit they are in torment but they don't know why. It was amazing to see how many of the students we met with in the campus ministry came in and said, "I don't know why I'm here. I really don't know if I need to forgive someone, but I felt like I needed to talk to you." As we worked through the Protocols of Forgiveness, it became clear to them what wounds they needed to forgive.

We come across people every day who are carrying old wounds and suffering some degree of torment because of their unforgiveness. For example, as I was editing this chapter in a doctor's office, the nurse taking my vitals opened up to me about her need to forgive herself. I truly believe if we learn to recognize the signs and become skilled in the Protocols of Forgiveness, we could deliver a forgiveness miracle every day.

So, are you ready to join the *Forgiveness Revolution*? Are you ready to learn how to *Forgive Forward*? If you are, I promise your life will never be the same. I can say that with confidence because God has established a protocol wherein forgiveness always brings a miracle of deliverance. So, to help you join the *Forgiveness Revolution*, we are going to teach you how to recognize the signs of unforgiveness in someone's life and to gently open their heart in order to gain access to their sacred place—the place they keep the private things of their soul.

### RECOGNIZING THE SIGNS

If we are to help set people free from torment, a few questions arise: "How do you know if someone is being tormented? Are there signs of unforgiveness in a person's life and demeanor that are recognizable?" I believe there are recognizable signs that notify us of unforgiveness in ourselves and others. Let's look again at Ephesians 4:31-32. *"Let all bitterness and wrath and anger and clamor and slander be put away from you, along with all malice. Be kind to one another, tender-hearted, forgiving each other, just as God in Christ also has forgiven you."*

In this passage Paul identifies the clues of unforgiveness. Look for bitterness, wrath, anger, clamor, slander and malice. Bitterness is the overarching category under which the other clues fall. The word bitterness here is "a figurative term denoting an irritable state of mind that keeps a man in perpetual animosity—that inclines him to harsh and uncharitable opinions of men and things—that makes him sour, crabby and repulsive in his general demeanor—that brings a scowl over his face and infuses venom into the words of his tongue."[7] Bitterness carries the connotation of something rancid and distasteful. The other six descriptive terms for bitterness fall into three categories: disposition, speech and actions. Disposition refers to the face, body language and the overall demeanor of a person. Speech refers to the words people use in discussions with or about the other party. Actions are what people do in response to or toward the person who wounded them. Bitterness always affects how we look, what we say and what we do.

## Bitterness always affects how we look, what we say and what we do.

### DISPOSITION CLUES

The disposition clues are wrath and anger. The word "wrath" means "burning rage, to snort." A wrathful person's disposition is loud and passionately explosive and, in most cases, temporary. Euphemisms for someone full of wrath are "He lost his cool" or "She lost her temper." (The "I lost my temper" statement is particularly amusing to me. When I hear someone say this, I'm tempted to say, "Well I think I may know exactly where it is.") The second word "anger" refers to the more subtle and abiding sense of anger. It's quiet anger. It simmers just below the surface and is often covered with a smile that doesn't seem sincere. You know the look. A smile that is on the mouth but not in the eyes. This type of anger is more acceptable socially, but is more deceptive than the concept of wrath. At least when someone blows up in anger you know where they stand. Stealth anger is long-term and most damaging to the one who carries it.

### SPEECH CLUES

The speech clues are similar to the disposition clues in that one is loud and one is quiet. The word "clamor" refers to an outcry, shouting, screaming, or "a cry of strife." Clamor refers to loud angry words and shouting between members of the body or group. It's a boisterous argument. We have all seen clamor displayed at town hall meetings, political rallies and, all too often, in church meetings and behind closed doors at home. Clamor is an unbridled use of the tongue to verbally tear down the character of someone else. It is public verbal vengeance. The second speech clue "slander" refers to profane and abusive speech but with the genteel twist. Slander is stealth verbal anger. In their book "Seeking Solid Ground," John Trent and Rick Hicks define slander as "gathering inside information on a co-worker, friend, or loved one and twisting it with others in order to do the person serious harm."[8] Slander is distorting the truth in such a way that leads people to believe a lie about someone.

Do you know that everything that is true is not the truth? Let me illustrate. In Chapter One, I told you about a visit Toni and I made to my parents' house to help them remodel one of their bathrooms. My dad loved coffee and my mom still does. For as long as I can remember, my folks have had a coffee pot set on a timer to brew first thing in the morning. When one pot is empty, they brew another one. Sometimes in the middle of the day they may switch to decaf, but there's always coffee in my parents' house. We drove the 400-mile trip from Atlanta to Paducah, Kentucky to help them with a project and not one time did my mother offer me a cup of coffee. She offered coffee to Toni several times, but not to me. They totally ignored me with coffee offers. Does that seem hospitable to you? What kind of mother does not offer coffee to her son when he comes home to help her? Would it be helpful for you know that my mother knows I don't drink coffee and she made sure I had all the tea and diet soda I wanted? You see what I said was true, but it led you away from the truth. Mom not offering me coffee was an act of love, not an act of disrespect. Slander takes what is true and distorts it so that someone believes a lie. When you hear someone say things about another person that don't seem right, there's a good chance unforgiveness is at play.

### ACTION CLUES

The action clue is "malice" which refers to "badness, wickedness, trouble." It is from the root word which means: evil, outworking of evil, evil advice, maliciousness. Malice is taking our bitter attitude and bitter words and putting them into action. Notice the progression? Bitterness affects a person's mood and disposition. If it's not addressed quickly, bitterness seeps into our conversations—snide remarks, sarcasm and unhealthy comments toward the offending party. Bitter people want others to know what happened to them and take their side in the matter. That's how I noticed Dad's unforgivenes in the story I shared in Chapter One. When he spoke about his friends, you could hear the bitterness and "grrrr" in his voice. That's why God had me speak to him. If the bitter speech is not addressed, the bitterness can ultimately lead to acts of vengeance. Bitterness taken to its extreme can ultimately lead to murder. In cases where someone harbors unforgiveness toward themselves for extended periods of time, you will see self-destructive behavior that can ultimately lead to suicide. As we discovered with Roger, addictive behavior is self-destructive because it's an expression of self-vengeance. People who have not forgiven themselves and are angry with themselves often engage in self-destructive behavior as a form of self-punishment. If something bad happens to them, they think they deserve it.

When you see these signs of bitterness, there's a good chance you have an assignment from God. Feel intimidated? Don't worry. God has provided the resource and strategy for your success. Keep reading. The next two chapters will show you how. It's easier than you may think.

CHAPTER EIGHT

# The Protocols of Forgiveness

▸▸

In writing *Forgiving Forward* we have shared several stories with you that illustrate the transformational impact forgiveness has on people. In the past year alone, we have literally seen hundreds of people set free. I like the way one woman described her life after forgiveness. "The only way I know how to put it into words is, 'I feel alive again.'" We share these stories to show the limitless opportunities to deliver forgiveness miracles. Our goal in writing this book is for you to (1) learn how to forgive, (2) be trained to help someone else forgive and (3) be trained to teach others how to help someone else forgive. That's how the *Forgiveness Revolution* expands. The stories we've shared are fresh and current. But the Protocols of Forgiveness can be traced all the way back to the beginning of humankind.

One of the most well known stories of forgiveness is found in Genesis 37-50. It's the story of Joseph and his brothers. Jacob had 12 sons. Joseph was the second to the youngest—Jacob's favorite. I know, I know…fathers aren't supposed to have favorites. If you ask the experts, parents are expected to love all their children the same. But most children think their parents have favorites and, if you ask them, it's always the other sibling. In Joseph's case, he really was the favorite. Jacob had given him a special coat signifying the favoritism not only to Joseph, but also to everyone else. Evidently, God liked Joseph a lot too. We know this because God gave Joseph two dreams, both interpreted to mean that Joseph's brothers would bow down to him sometime in the future. It's pretty cool for a young kid to find out from God that all of his brothers were going to yield and submit to him. This would fall into the "way cool" category for anyone, unless of course you were one of the older brothers.

Joseph made the huge mistake of telling his brothers about the dreams and what they meant. If you are the favorite, it's never a good idea to point it out to your brothers because there's zero percent chance it will go over well when you do. I'm not sure what Joseph expected his brothers' reaction to be. If he expected them to be happy for him—predictably, they weren't.

Sometime later, when Joseph went to check on his brothers as they worked, they seized the opportunity to get rid of their problem for good. They grabbed Joseph, threw him in a pit, then debated what to do with him. Most of the brothers wanted to kill him, but instead they sold him to a band of gypsies passing by on their way to Egypt. This would not be in the "way cool" category. The brothers took Joseph's special coat, poured blood all over it and showed it to Jacob. "Dad, we found this coat. It looks like Joseph's. What do you think?" They led their father to believe his favorite son was dead, so Jacob wouldn't send out a search party to find Joseph. They would be free from the annoying little brat forever, or so they thought.

As the saga continues, the gypsies sold Joseph to a man named Potiphar, a high-ranking official in the Egyptian army. Since he was still one of God's favorites, Joseph rose quickly to become the house manager for Potiphar's estate. He oversaw everything that Potiphar owned and all the other servants reported to him. Unfortunately, Mrs. P. got the "hots" for Joseph. She tried to seduce him. Several times! He resisted. Several times! She grabbed him.

He ran away. She cried "rape!" He got arrested and thrown in the royal prison.

But God's favor was still on Joseph. While in prison for an act he did not commit, the chief jailer put him in charge of everything. Joseph interpreted a couple of dreams for a couple of prisoners, both of which came true. Years later, Pharaoh had a couple of dreams that no one could interpret. One of the guys from prison told Pharaoh about Joseph's ability to interpret dreams. Pharaoh called for Joseph and he interpreted Pharaoh's dreams. The dreams predicted there would be seven years of bumper crops followed by seven years of no crops. Pharaoh was to save all of the extra grain from the seven good years so they would have plenty in the seven lean years. Egypt could sell grain to the rest of the world who ran out of food during the famine. Pharaoh was so impressed, he elevated Joseph to the position of prime minister of Egypt, the number two man in the entire nation. Since Egypt was the only superpower of the day, Joseph suddenly was the second most powerful man in the world. God took Joseph from being sold by his brothers to gypsies to being the man in charge of the world's food supply. Pretty amazing.

> **You see, that's not what happens when you sell little brothers to gypsies. That is, unless God intervenes.**

Everything happened as Joseph predicted. During the famine years, Egypt had plenty when the rest of the world ran out of food. So guess who got hungry? Big brothers. Dad (Jacob) sent big brothers to Egypt to buy food. Guess who they had to buy the food from? Little brother. But they didn't recognize him. How could they? I mean, come on, if you put your little brother in a pit and sell him as a slave to gypsies, then later you run out of food, go to Egypt and see the guy in charge of the food supply for the whole world, you're not going to say "Hey, that's our little brother." I can imagine the brothers, when they saw Joseph, saying to one another "Doesn't he remind you of—naaa, couldn't be." You see, that's not what happens when you sell little brothers to gypsies. That is, unless God intervenes.

Joseph eventually revealed himself to his big brothers and provided them with all the food they needed. With Pharaoh's permission, Joseph brought his Dad and entire family to Egypt and placed them in the land of Goshen, which was the best land in all of Egypt. There was plenty of room for the entire family and all their herds and flocks. Joseph blessed his family with everything they needed and more.

Eventually Jacob died, and the brothers were filled with fear. They wondered if Joseph showed such compassion only because of Dad. Now with Dad gone, they were afraid that Joseph would finally enact vengeance upon them (think Michael Corleone at the end of *Godfather I.*) They jumped to conclusions and assumed they were in big trouble. Who wouldn't think that?

> *So they sent a message to Joseph, saying, "Your father charged before he died, saying, 'Thus you shall say to Joseph, 'Please forgive, I beg you, the transgression of your brothers and their sin, for they did you wrong. And now, please forgive the transgression of the servants of the God of your father'." And Joseph wept when they spoke to him. Then his brothers also came and fell down before him and said, "Behold, we are your servants." But Joseph said to them, "Do not be afraid, for am I in God's place. As for you, you meant evil against me, but God meant it for good in order to bring about this present result, to preserve many people alive. So therefore, do not be afraid; I will provide for you and your little ones." So he comforted them and spoke kindly to them. (Genesis 50:16-21)*

Did you notice what happened? The brothers came in Dad's name and admitted that what they did to him so many years before was wrong. That sounds like repentance doesn't it? Joseph's reaction was emotional. He wept. (When you have forgiven and yearn for reconciliation, it can be emotional when the offending party comes to you in repentance.)

Joseph's response to their repentance displays an incredible insight that is key in helping people learn how to forgive. He said, "Do not be afraid, for am I in God's place?" Joseph knew his place in the Kingdom order, and he understood that ultimately God is sovereign over everything and everyone, including brothers who sell their little brother to a band of gypsies. He went on to say, "You meant evil against me, but God meant it for good in order to bring about this present result, to preserve many people alive." Please note that Joseph didn't say, "It's okay big brothers. It's no big deal. It doesn't matter." It wasn't okay. What they did was wrong. *Forgiveness does not devalue the wound or the damage caused.* On the contrary, forgiveness acknowledges the pain and the hurt but simply chooses not to hold it against the offender.

Joseph's declaration is the Old Testament equivalent to Romans 8:28. *"And we know that God causes all things to work together for good to those who love God, to those who are called according to His purpose."* This text does not say God causes all things. He does not. If He did, He would be guilty of causing sin. God's holiness means that He is completely incapable of creating sinful activities. He is totally free from evil of any kind. What this text does say is that God causes all things to *work together* for good. He does not participate *in* sin, but He participates *with* sin to bring about His glory and our good. God is brilliant at taking man's screwups, whether intentional or not, and using them to fulfill His predetermined purposes. Here's a question for you: if Joseph's brothers had not sold him to the band of gypsies, would he still have been elevated to the position in Egypt that allowed him to rescue his family, God's people, from starvation? We don't know for sure but I believe the answer is "yes." I believe God would have used another plan and other circumstances to fulfill the dreams He gave Joseph when he was a child. The prediction that his brothers would bow down to him occurred long before the brothers decided to sell Joseph. People's sins against us do not change God's ultimate plan for us; it just affects the pathway to the fulfillment of the plan.

**Focusing on God reminds us to embrace the blessings in the pain, rather than reacting in retaliation.**

The brothers sinned grievously, but Joseph forgave them. Joseph had a higher understanding of God's ability to take bad situations and transform them for God's glory and his ultimate good. It changes everything when your focus is on God, His power and His sovereignty. It does not excuse the pain inflicted, but focusing on God reminds us that He can redeem it. We've been hurt very deeply at various times in our lives. Toni and I would never choose to go through the pain of the betrayals, slander and abandonment we've endured again. However, we cherish the blessings and growth we gained through each and every one of them. We witnessed and experienced the amazing redemptive power of God over and over again through the darkest periods of our lives. That's why we can say with confidence that while God doesn't cause everything, He does redeem everything by causing all to work together for His glory and our good. That's why we are careful not to allow someone's sin to cause us to sin. Focusing on God reminds us to embrace the blessings in the pain, rather than reacting in retaliation. This focus is the foundation of our ability to forgive.

Why is God's sovereignty important to the process of helping other people forgive? Helping others look at the greater picture changes their perspective regarding the piece of the puzzle they're living. When we realize the actions of others in attempting to undo us ultimately cooperates with God's plan to fashion us into everything He's designed us to be, it's easy to forgive their actions against us. Understanding God's providence and grace motivates us to forgive and understanding God's Protocols of Forgiveness helps us know how to forgive.

Protocols are the rules or conventions of correct behavior in official or ceremonial occasions. Kingdoms and governments function with a set of recognized procedures that govern how things are accomplished. In the Kingdom of Heaven there are certain protocols associated with forgiveness. There's nothing magical to the words we use. We've found that there's a basic order of forgiving that works most effectively, although we have sometimes switched up the order based upon the leading of the Spirit at the time. We do, however, find that if these seven protocols are processed with a willing heart, a freedom miracle takes place automatically. Remember God withholds His protection when someone does not forgive and He unleashes His protection when we do. So let's learn the seven Protocols of Forgiveness.

### 7 PROTOCOLS OF FORGIVENESS

We have found it is most effective to walk through the 7 Protocols of Forgiveness "aloud." *"Therefore, confess your sins to one another, and pray for one another so that you may be healed. The effective prayer of a righteous man can accomplish much"* (James 5:16). As you are coaching someone through these protocols, ask them to speak them aloud. If you are using these protocols personally, ask someone you trust to be a witness as you declare your forgiveness aloud. There is something that occurs in the spiritual realm when we confess our sins to one another. The Bible is not clear on whether God's enemy and his demonic helpers can read our minds. It is clear they can hear our voices. Confessing your forgiveness verbally will help you when you get to Protocol 6.

### 1. Thank God for forgiving you.

Does praise follow freedom or does freedom follow praise? The connection between praise and freedom may be the classic "which comes first" question. Is it the chicken or the egg? When we reflect on how much God has forgiven us, we are all-the-more eager to forgive others. Pride says, "I would never commit that sin." Yet the truth remains that we are all capable of sin at any level. Let's face it; we *all* mess up but God loves us anyway.

If you can help someone redirect their focus to God's graciousness to them, you will see a dramatic reduction in their emotions against the person who has offended them. We have found an effective tool in helping move people from complaint to praise. When someone shares with us a complaint against someone else, we often ask a series of simple questions. The conversation goes something like this:

"What did he do?"

"He lied to me."

"That must really hurt. I hate it when someone lies to me."

"It makes me so angry."

"I can see that. Have you ever lied to someone?"

"What?"

"Have you ever lied?"

"Well…yes…I have."

"How did you want to be treated when you lied? Do you want to be marked by that? We all make mistakes, don't we? Aren't you glad God is gracious to us when we do things like this? Why don't we praise Him for His grace toward us?"

It is amazing how transformational that type of conversation can be for someone who is hurting. Praise puts everything in proper perspective and produces a humility that opens the door for forgiveness.

### 2. Ask God, "Who do I need to forgive and for what?"

Most of the time determining who needs to be forgiven does not take long. By the time you have moved people toward allowing you to coach them through forgiveness, the person and the offense becomes evident. If you're not sure, use probing questions like: "Is there one event in your life that seems to haunt you?" "In your life, who has wounded you the greatest?" "What has happened in your life that has brought you the most pain?"

Sometimes the situation requires prioritizing and ordering the wounds. Silently pray to God and ask Him to clarify to the person where to start. Which wound needs forgiveness first? It's important to note, some people's wounds are too numerous to deal with all at once. I believe that there are key unforgiveness issues that God associates with the torment for each person. There are certain wounds, often from early in life or from people closest to us, that are the primary reason for our torment. These core wounds need to be forgiven first. We have found when these core wounds are dealt with first, lesser wounds become unimportant. You will be amazed how God will consistently give clarity and revelation at this point in the process. This protocol of asking God who needs to be forgiven and what they need to be forgiven for invites God into the process and provides wisdom as we move to the next protocol. As you are coaching them, help them to stay focused on one offender at a time as you walk through Protocols 3-5.

### 3. Repent of your sin of unforgiveness.

Unforgiveness is a sin. I know, I know. It doesn't feel like a sin. But it really is important that the person you're helping comes to grip with this truth. Often the response we hear to this protocol is something like: "*They* hurt *me*." "It wasn't *my* fault. "It's *my* choice whether I forgive or not." "I have a right to be upset. They owe me." While all of those feelings are understandable, unforgiveness is still a sin, and it's the sin that keeps people in torment.

Recently a young man asked to meet with me to talk about his relationship with his father. What he described to me was the very definition of dysfunctional. The wounds were so deep that this young man refused to use the names "Father" or "Dad" and asked me to call his father by his first name, Jim. You could read the torment in his face and body language.

We discussed several Bible passages that show how important forgiveness is to God and how He views our unforgiveness as sin. The young man was resistant to confessing this, so I moved on, planning to address it later. As we began to walk through the process of forgiving "Jim," I sensed there was still a block. He said, "I choose to forgive Ji..." and wasn't able to continue. So

**Unforgiveness is not just a bad idea; it is sin. Unless you repent of this way of thinking, you will not be free.**

I said to him, "You still think you have a choice whether to forgive or not, don't you? You think you are doing Jim a favor by forgiving him, don't you? You need to confess your sin of unforgiveness toward Jim because forgiveness is not an option. *Unforgiveness is not just a bad idea; it is sin.* Unless you repent of this way of thinking, you will not be free."

What happened next is unforgettable. This young man said, "Lord, I repent of my sin of unforgiveness toward Ji... toward Ji... toward my dad." And with that, he broke, and the tears began to flow. Without my prompting, he began to forgive his dad for every single wound he could remember. He never used the name "Jim" again. From that time on, he talked about his "dad." It was incredible to watch love and compassion toward his father replace the torment. You see, until we recognize that unforgiveness is a sin, we will view it as an option. And as long as we view it as an option, we will feel justified in our unforgiveness. As long as we feel justified in our unforgiveness, we will not repent of it and we will be bound to the torment that goes with it. But when we confess our unforgiveness as sin, we are set free, just like my young friend.

### 4. Forgive each offense from your heart.

Now is the time to walk them through forgiveness. At this point lead the forgiver through a short prayer. Begin with something like, "Heavenly Father, I'm here with Your son (or daughter) and he has something to say that I know thrills Your heart. Please listen to him and set him free as he yields to You in this act of forgiveness." At this point they take the active role and you take the coaching role by having them walk through the following:

a. *"Lord, I choose to forgive _____ _____, from my heart, for _____.*

It is important to remember we forgive wounds, not people in general. We forgive people for the individual wounds they have caused. It's not enough to say, "I forgive my dad" or "I forgive my mom." That is simply not specific enough. Jesus always separated the person from his sin. He forgave people for sins. Jesus loved the sinner but hated their sin. We are to maintain the same mindset. We make sure those we lead through forgiveness forgive the wounds and the actions that caused their pain, not just the people. Once the process begins, we have found the words of forgiveness will flow. With the first couple of wounds we may have to coach them a little, but once they start to truly forgive, the Holy Spirit partners with us and leads them. He will bring to their minds the things He wants them to forgive. All we need to do is be quiet and alert. Most of the time when there is a pause, all we have to do is to ask the question, "Is there anything else?" The Holy Spirit is the true Coach in this process and will bring it to completion. He will tell us when to conclude this section. We will just know because He will make it clear to us. When we sense this part is winding down, we coax them by suggesting they ask God the following confirmation question:

b. *"Lord, is there anything else I need to forgive _____ for?"*

Remember, forgiveness is a decision, not a process. Forgiveness sometimes feels more like a process than a decision because we often have to forgive a series of wounds, just like a movie is a series of still shots shown quickly over light. It sometimes takes a long time to remember and deal with the multiple offenses someone has committed against us. What feels like a process to someone is simply a series of decisions they must make regarding another person's actions against them.

Don't be afraid of silence at this point. The Holy Spirit uses the silence to work in the heart of the forgiver. Our Divine Partner in this forgiveness miracle is more than capable of communicating clearly to the person we're coaching. He also knows just how much this person can handle at a time. Oftentimes the wounded individual has been hurt so many times by so many people it would be too intense to deal with it all at once. The Holy Spirit knows which wounds to address first. Frequently, the secondary wounds stem from the primary ones. Sometimes God deals with just a few at a time by not allowing the person to remember all of the wounds they have suffered. Torment ends anyway, because God honors the act of faith necessary to be willing to forgive, and the miracle of forgiveness takes place.

When the forgiver says, "I don't remember anything else," simply affirm them by saying "Good." Tell them there may be more things that God reminds them of later. Assure them that it's OK if they haven't covered it all right now because they now know what to do if more memories come back. Then encourage them to make the forgiveness declaration:

> c. *"Before God, I declare* _____ *is no longer in my debt."*

At this point the process of forgiveness is coming to a close. It's time to officially transfer the debt of the wound to the cross of Jesus Christ. By making it official, almost like a symbolic ceremony, the burden is lifted. The costs do not disappear, but rather transfer out of our account and into the account of the cross. It's similar to our mortgage. The current mortgage holder of our house is not the company who extended the loan. All the terms and conditions of the loan are the same with the exception of where we send the payment. The first lender sold it to a different company. The original company no longer has legal right to approach us for repayment of the debt. To do so would be fraudulent. The debt has been transferred to another. In the same way, when we forgive someone and transfer the debt to the cross, it's up to the Lord of the cross to settle accounts with them.

Having forgiven and declared the offending party to be no longer in their debt, it is now time to use what we call the "forgiveness validator."

### 5. Seal it with a blessing.

There is a clear and foolproof indicator that forgiveness has taken place. Forgiveness is sealed with a blessing. At this point, invite the person to ask God to bless the offending party and to look for ways to bless them when possible. We will know if someone has truly forgiven when they're willing to give a blessing to the one who has wounded them.

My friend Connie recently asked me, "Bruce, a few years ago our son-in-law stole some money from us. We have proof he did it but he's never admitted it. I think I've forgiven him, but every time we're in the same room together I'm really uncomfortable, and so is he. Am I missing something?"

I thought for moment and asked, "Have you blessed him? You know you have truly forgiven someone when you're willing to bless them."

"I've never thought of it that way. What do you suggest?"

I paused and prayed silently. I then sensed the Lord telling me to say, "Bless him in the area in which he violated you. Bless him financially."

"I know exactly what to do. I'm going to give him $500 because that's the amount he stole from us."

I saw her a few days later and asked what happened. She told me she gave her son-in-law $500 cash and told him he couldn't use it to pay bills. She wanted him to use it on something for himself that he wouldn't be able to afford otherwise. She told him she loved him and was sorry for the distance she had allowed to exist between them. I asked her how he responded. She said, "He just shrugged his shoulders, mumbled 'thanks' and walked away."

**Blessing those who have wounded us is what seals the forgiveness.**

"Did that hurt?" I asked.

"No, my heart was free. The blessing was for me. I'm free whether he is or not."

Blessing those who have wounded us is what seals the forgiveness and proves that we are free. It is the undeniable proof we have laid down the desire for vengeance and have forgiven. Unforgiveness demands vengeance. Forgiveness desires blessing. Blessing honors God. God honors blessing.

### 6. Commit to "not remember" the offense.

The enemy of God loves to remind us of the forgiven wounds. The emotions attached to those wounds sometimes take a while to settle and die out. So the enemy reminds those who have forgiven of their old wounds with distracting whispers like, "How can you forget that?" or "That really did hurt, didn't it? Are you sure you want to let that go?" He is a master at his role as "the accuser of the brethren."

Many people believe that since they continue to 'remember' the offense, they must have not forgiven. Remember forgiveness does not say what happened did not matter or that it did not happen. Forgiveness does not change the reality of the event, just our response to it. We really cannot choose to forget something, but we can strategize to make sure we don't remember, (i.e. dwell on it). Let me explain what I mean. Picture in your mind's eye your favorite reading spot: a quiet corner of the room, a beach, a porch in the mountains. Imagine off to your right side there is an elephant in a pink tutu, dancing. Can you see it? She is up on her toes doing a perfect pirouette. Do you have the visual? Now forget about it. I want you to stop thinking about the elephant in the pink tutu that is spinning over there. You can't do it, can you? The only way you can forget about something is by choosing "not to remember" and focusing on something else. So as you are coaching someone, here are some tools to help them deal with the memories when they resurface.

When the memory comes…

### a. Say, "I specifically remember forgiving that."

So the enemy can hear you, restate out loud, "I have already forgiven that."

### b. Praise God for the freedom forgiveness brought you.

Everyone who confesses their sin of unforgiveness and chooses to forgive a person who has wounded them will receive a heart miracle. Whenever we've delivered a forgiveness miracle we always ask the question, "How's your heart?" Without fail, we hear something like this: "My heart is light." "I feel free." "My heart is calm." We have even heard "My heart is fluffy." As a guy, I'm not sure what that means, but I know it's good. One person told me that she felt like she had just exhaled for the first time in months. When the enemy brings the memory of the wound back to you, use it as an occasion to praise God for the release that happened when you forgave. This frustrates the work of the enemy.

### c. Bless the person you forgave— again.

Remember the opposite of a vengeful attitude is a blessing attitude. You already blessed the person when you forgave. Repeating the blessing takes you back to the attitude of Christ toward the person. I promise when someone chooses to praise God and bless the other person each time the enemy attempts to bring the memory of the wound to them, the enemy will eventually leave them alone about the issue. How can I guarantee that? Because the two things the enemy of our souls hates the most is when God's people praise Him and when they bless those who hurt them. *"Bless those who curse you, pray for those who mistreat you." (Luke 6:28)* If we can demonstrate to him that this is what we will do every time the memory comes, he will leave us alone.

### d. Pray for reconciliation.

We discussed the difference between forgiveness, repentance and reconciliation in Chapter Six. Our role in reconciliation is to forgive. We cannot control whether or not the offending party ever comes to repentance (i.e. changes their mind about the situation.) The only influence we have on this is through prayer and bless-ing. Personally, Toni and I have been hurt by many people, some of whom were very close friends. We have made a commitment to pray for them regularly that God would bless them and, by the grace of God and in His timing, we might

**Pre-forgiveness is choosing daily not to receive an offense but rather taking every relational debt and transferring it immediately to the cross.**

be reconciled to them. We know the best thing we can do is pray and leave it in God's hands and in theirs. This is true for you and the person you are helping as well.

### 7. Make pre-forgiveness a lifestyle.

Just like preventative medicine is the best medicine, pre-forgiveness is the best kind of forgiveness. When protocol 7 is followed, the need for the other six is greatly diminished, if not eliminated. We've learned the secret of pre-forgiveness. Pre-forgiveness is choosing daily not to receive an offense but rather taking every relational debt and transferring it immediately to the cross. The blood of Jesus covers all sin including the ones committed against me. It also includes the ones that haven't happened yet. Really? Really!!!

I have a friend who wakes up every morning looks at his wife of over 30 years and says, "I forgive you for anything you do today that offends me, hurts me, or in any way would tick me off. And you have my permission to remind me of this promise at any time." I have to tell you this couple has one the most amazing, fun relationships of any couple I know. When we cultivate and develop a mindset of forgiveness, we find our life is full of joy. Pre-forgiveness is the vaccination against torment.

CHAPTER NINE

# Gaining Access to Their Sacred Place
▸▸

I have some great news for you. Your assignment, should you choose to accept it, is not difficult. It's impossible. That's right. Our assignment is impossible –if we try to do it alone. God never intended for us to deliver His miracles alone. He promised we would be given a Partner, a supernatural One at that, to help us accomplish our task. And our Partner is smarter, stronger, more capable and much more interested in the success of the mission than we are. Our Partner is none other than the Holy Spirit Himself.

When Jesus returned to the Father He promised He would not leave us on our own. Here's what He says:

> *"I will ask the Father, and He will give you another Helper, that He may be with you forever; that is the Spirit of truth, whom the world cannot receive, because it does not see Him or know Him, but you know Him because He abides with you and will be in you. I will not leave you as orphans." (John 14:16-18a)*

> *"But when He, the Spirit of truth, comes, He will guide you into all the truth; for He will not speak on His own initia-*

*tive, but whatever He hears, He will speak; and He will*
*disclose to you what is to come. He will glorify Me, for*
*He will take of Mine and will disclose it to you." (John*
*16:13-14)*

The God of Heaven is so concerned about our success in *The*
*Forgiveness Revolution* that He promised He, in the person of the
Holy Spirit, will team with us to set people free. So while our task
is impossible on our own, our success is guaranteed when we team
up with our Divine Partner.

The beauty of the system is this: God knows who He wants to
set free, how He wants it done, when He wants it done and who He
wants to help Him. He does all the planning and all the finishing.
Our job is simply to be on alert for His signals, to listen for His
instructions and to say and do what He tells us to say and do. In
fact, when you engage in a forgiveness miracle, the only way you
can mess it up is to try to do it on your own. However, when you
partner with the God of Heaven, amazing things can happen. My
friend John found this to be true.

### JOHN'S STORY

John is a business coach who travels around the country
helping executives and corporations maximize their potential.
Several months ago he traveled with us on a mission trip to
Central America where I taught the Protocols of Forgiveness to
pastors and ministry leaders. One of the ministry opportunities
for our team was to speak to a group of high school students
about Christ. We provided a pizza party for the students so our
team could connect with them. Fresh off of hearing the *Forgiving*
*Forward* message, John (through a translator and the direction of
the Holy Spirit) was able to connect with a young man and lead
him through the Protocols of Forgiveness. This student forgave
his father for the wounds inflicted upon him. John also had an opportunity to team up with Toni to help a young lady find freedom
through forgiveness. As Toni led Maria through forgiveness for

a number of atrocious acts committed against her by her father, she was impressed by the Holy Spirit to ask John to step in as a man of God and pray a fatherly blessing over her. Toni paused her prayer and went to ask John if he would come join them. He agreed, and as he began to pray for this young lady, he heard the Holy Spirit tell him to stand in the place of her father and ask for her forgiveness. With the impact of John's words, she was able to forgive her father for all the wrong he had done. John then prayed a blessing over her. Later, when Toni and John were about to leave the high school, Maria came up to them, took the ribbon out of her hair and handed it to Toni. "This is for you. It is all I have. Please remember me." Then she reached in her pocket, pulled out a very small picture of herself and handed it to John. She asked, "Can I be your El Salvadorian granddaughter?" John embraced Maria in tears.

When I saw John later that night he looked like he'd just won the lottery or kicked the winning field goal in the Super Bowl. He was so pumped. He said, "Bruce, I did it. I helped two young people find freedom by forgiving their dads. Wow!"

After we returned home, John went on a business trip to coach a client in another state. He called me one evening and told me he sensed God wanted him to help a young man at his client's firm. "Bruce, he's one of the up-and-coming leaders in this organization, but something is blocking him. I sense it's a forgiveness issue. How do I gain entrance into his heart so I can help him?" I coached him through the protocols of opening someone's heart and helping them forgive (which we will teach you in this chapter.) I prayed with him for God to make his way clear and successful. He promised he'd let me know what happened.

A few days later John called and told me the story of an amazing breakthrough in this executive's life. John helped this man uncover an old wound from years ago, buried deep inside his heart. This unforgiven wound brought torment. John then led him through the Protocols of Forgiveness. The man confessed his sin of unforgiveness and forgave the wound he had carried for so long. A few months later I asked John how this guy was doing. Not only is his heart free, but his effectiveness as a corporate leader is skyrocketing. He has helped set family members free from unforgiveness as well as co-workers in the organization. On top of that he told John, "We need to strategize together how we can help the people in our company become free from the wounds of their past. Not only will this benefit them, but it will also help our company reach its fullest potential."

## Our heart is the place where we keep the memories of special blessings and painful wounds.

If you were to ask John what the secret to his success was, he would tell you that it is his depending upon the Holy Spirit more so than following the protocols. Yet, it does require both a total dependence upon the Holy Spirit *and* following the patterns God has established. My friend Mike Wells likes to say, "All that Jesus did, He never did. The One who did everything, did nothing." What he means is Jesus only did what the Father told Him to do through the power given to Him by the Holy Spirit. Therefore we are never to do anything on our own either. We should only do what Jesus tells us to do through the power He gives us by the Holy Spirit. The Holy Spirit will guide us into all truth. He will open doors for us. He is the One who will open the hearts of the people to whom He sends us. He is the One who actually provides the miracle. We need to always keep in mind that we are simply the delivery agents. We are only to follow the plan of God in the power of God. Nothing more, nothing less.

### What is the Sacred Place?

This is never truer than when it comes to gaining access to a person's sacred place where they store the wounds of the past. When we use the term "sacred place" we are referring to a person's heart. Our heart is the place where we keep the memories of special blessings and painful wounds. While techniques are important, only the Holy Spirit can open a person's heart. The unforgiven wounds are always wounds of the heart. Heart wounds cut deep and are held very close. People don't hurt our heads; they hurt our hearts. When people say, "I have a headache," we offer them an aspirin. When people say, "My heart aches," we assume it's emotional, not physical, and we ask, "What's going on?" Disagreements of the mind are simply disagreements. Disagreements of the heart are a whole different matter.

Remember what we used to say as kids. "Sticks and stones may break my bones, but words will never hurt me." Well this statement is just not true—it's a defense mechanism to keep people from seeing into our hearts. Do you remember saying it as a kid? Do you recall the urge to cry afterwards when no one could see you? We all did this. The truth is words can hurt our hearts—deeply. There is a bitter irony to the way we manage our most intimate pain. We tend to bury our hurts deep inside of ourselves and protect them like they are precious jewels. Unfortunately, the wounds are not jewels; they are seeds of a cancer that will eat away the very thing we are trying to protect—our hearts.

In the Bible the heart refers to the seat or center of a person's emotions and spiritual life. The heart is where our thoughts, emotions, passions and life connections originate. It is in our hearts we make our core decisions about what we believe. Romans 10:8-10 clarifies this. *"But what does it say? 'The word is near you, in your mouth and in your heart'—that is, the word of faith which we are preaching, that if you confess with your mouth Jesus as Lord, and believe in your heart that God raised Him from the dead, you will be saved; for with the heart a person believes, resulting in righteousness, and with the mouth he confesses, resulting in salvation."* We receive information with our minds; we embrace truth with our hearts. This is why Paul prayed that the *"eyes of your hearts may be enlightened so that you may know what is the hope of His calling, what are the riches of the glory of His inheritance in the saints, and what is the surpassing greatness of His power to us who believe"* (Ephesians 1:18-19a). If you do not connect with a person's heart, you will not help him forgive.

### AN UNOPENED HEART

The importance of connecting with a person's heart was re-affirmed to me recently. I arranged a meeting with someone wounded by a mutual friend. He experienced a crushing heart wound, and the effects spread to his entire family. The signs of bitterness and unforgiveness were clear to those who knew the situation. I sensed in my spirit an assignment from the Lord. I was to intervene in a Galatians 6:1 way with this man and his family. My goal was not to excuse the behavior of the offender, but rather to help this person and his family become free through the power of forgiveness. We met at a coffee shop and exchanged the usual pleasantries. I then broached the subject by expressing concern for the family and told him I believed God wanted them to forgive the other person. I shared with him the insights the Lord had given us regarding the principle of torment from Matthew 18. We had what

**Information exchange does not produce transformation.**

I would call a nice polite conversation, which ended pleasantly. The man assured me he would process the information and thanked me for my concern. As I drove away from the coffee shop, I was disappointed that I didn't witness the break-through I'd seen so consistently when I presented this message to others. I asked the Lord, "What happened? Why didn't this work?" God's Spirit showed me I didn't connect with the man's heart. We came close once, but we never got to the point where we communicated heart to heart. I engaged his mind and he received the information as I presented it. But information exchange does not produce transformation. I tried too hard to convince him, and, in so doing, got in the way of the Holy Spirit's role.

As I said earlier, God the Father is more concerned with the person being able to forgive than we are. That's why He has as-signed the Holy Spirit to partner with us. My mistake with the man in the coffee shop was that I tried to "close the deal" myself. But, you see, that's not our job. It really isn't. It is the Holy Spirit's job to convince people of their need to forgive. When we rely upon Him to do His work, we will always be successful. When we try to do His job for Him, like I did in this case, we'll always mess it up. This is why it's important to master the art of connecting with people's hearts. If we don't, we will not reach the wounds that need forgiveness—the heart is where we keep our wounds. This is true for all of us. There's a bit of finesse required in connecting with someone's wounded heart, but I want to assure you that you can do it.

> **Forgiveness is what heals all wounds, not time.**

## HEART-TO-HEART NOT HEAD-TO-HEAD

Gaining access to someone's heart can be tricky because wounded people often embrace a subtle deception. This deception is expressed in statements like, "If we just forget about the offense and put it out of our minds, everything will be fine." "Forget about it." "Time heals all wounds." Yet putting something out of the mind does not put it out of the heart. *Forgiveness is what heals all wounds, not time.* In fact, failure to deal with a wound, by simply ignoring it, stuffs it deeper into us and makes it more difficult and painful to resolve. It's like we have placed the wound in a lockbox and then protect the lockbox as if our life depends on it. Unfortunately, our heart gets locked up with the infected wound as well. You see, unforgiveness always involves a heart wound, not a head wound.

How can you tell when you're interacting with someone heart-to-heart rather than head-to-head? How do you know when someone is opening themselves up to let you take a peek in inside? There are clear signs you can look for to know if someone feels safe with you. One of the key indicators that you've gained access to someone's heart is the speed, level and tone of their speech. Generally speaking, when people talk out of their head they tend to speak faster with a higher pitch and volume. When someone talks fast and really high they are trying to move information quickly from their head to your head. Head information can be transferred quickly. That's because there is no emotional attachment with head knowledge. But when we're dealing with issues of the heart (where emotions are seated), the communication delivery system automatically slows down. A person speaks slower. They think through their answers before responding. They process their thoughts more deliberately so they will communicate more deliberately as well. If you're talking with someone and you suspect they have an unforgiveness issue, relax, slow down, and lower your voice. Your gentle voice and demeanor will encourage them to open their hearts. Your calmness will help them feel safe.

It is important that people feel safe with you if you want them to trust you with their deepest wounds. When you talk to their heads, when you speak fast and intense, you portray a spirit of debate, competition, superiority, or nervousness. When you talk to their hearts, when you lower your voice and pace, you portray the spirit of empathy and concern. People need to know you care about what they're saying and what they're feeling. And make no mistake, people can tell if you're faking it. If they sense you don't really care, they will not open up to you.

**When they have admitted they experience torment, you're on your way to delivering a miracle because acknowledging the torment opens the door to their heart.**

Let me be perfectly clear—you cannot help someone forgive if you are judgmental. It is important to communicate the forgiveness message without an attitude of superiority or judgment toward the person. Sometimes I tell my own story of torment caused by unforgiveness and how my friend James helped me. There is no shame in not knowing what you have never learned. We have all needed someone else to help us understand Biblical truth—the issues of torment and unforgiveness are no different. People will sometimes say, "I didn't know that," to which I say, "that's okay—no one does until they learn it." So, if you really have trouble with being judgmental, ask God to change your heart toward people and their failures. One way to maintain the right perspective is to thank God for His forgiveness of you. Thank Him for the benefits you have received by forgiving and be grateful that someone helped you learn to forgive. This perspective and practice of praise also protects you from the danger of becoming proud in the process.

## IDENTIFYING THE WOUND

When you sense you have connected with a person's heart, you can begin to uncover the wounds. It's important to determine who and what hurt them—the person and the specific wound. Sometimes the person will give you verbal hints and sometimes they will just blurt it out to you. Other times you may need to probe a little bit by asking leading questions. We often use what Dr. Bruce Wilkinson calls *the unforgiveness validator question.* "Would you say that you experience torment from time to time?"[9] I can't tell you how many times we have heard the answer, "Why yes, how did you know?" If the answer is yes, you know there is unforgiveness. When they have admitted they experience torment, you're on your way to delivering a miracle because acknowledging the torment opens the door to their heart.

Once they invite you into their sacred place, you can begin the process of identifying the wounds which are causing the torment. The best way to do this is by gently asking probing questions that lead the person to recognize the source of the torment. There are many good questions to help you at this point. Try these:

"Who in your life has wounded you the deepest?"

"What are two or three of the most painful experiences in your life?"

"Is there something in your past that haunts you? Tell me about it."

If you've done a good job making them feel safe, they will open up to you. When I ask people to tell me their deepest pains, I often begin by telling them that nothing they say will change how I think about them. It will, however, change how I help them. People open up when you ask these questions and assure them nothing they tell you will cause you to think less of them.

### You're Safe with Their Story

Don't be surprised when emotions well up inside of you as you listen to someone's story. We've heard some of the most horrific stories when people have described the wounds they have endured. At different times, some of these stories have caused us to feel grief, anger, sympathy and horror. As important as it is to let the person know you empathize with their story, it is just as important for them not to witness you being overwhelmed by your emotions. You may also be tempted to take up an offense for them. Do not do that. Your job is to help them forgive and you cannot do this if you join in their offense. Everyone who helps others forgive has to come to terms with how to handle information they receive from the ones they are helping. There's a temptation to carry the emotions associated with what you are hearing into the process of coaching them. It's easy to put yourself or someone close to you into this situation and relive it as if it had happened to you. There is a fine line between empathy for the person, and projecting yourself into the event. It is so easy to cross that line, particularly when you have a sensitive heart for people. But there are ways to stay objective while empathizing with the person who needs to forgive. We have found it very helpful to maintain an accurate understanding of the human condition. Sin is a very real part of life. Evil exists in the world and people are capable of doing horrific things to other people. If this were not true, Jesus would not have had to die. I must confess, at times it looks like evil is winning. But in spite of those appearances, Jesus *did* win on the cross, and it is important we maintain this perspective. Do we cry with people as we hear their stories? Yes. Do we say, "I'm sorry you had to endure this"? Yes. Do we get angry when we hear the graphic sins described? Sometimes. But the goal we always keep in the forefront of our minds is to see them set free through forgiveness.

One of my favorite shows of all time was the 70's hit *M\*A\*S\*H*. The show depicted life at the 4077th Mobile Army Surgical Hospital during the Korean War. Hawkeye, Trapper, BJ, Henry, Margaret and the rest of the characters had to deal with the never-ending supply of wounded soldiers coming through their camp. Much of the show was filmed in the operating room, where the characters worked long hours trying to save the lives and limbs of their patients. A recurring theme in the series was the difficulty of managing the carnage of war all around them while trying to help the wounded. What they faced at the *M\*A\*S\*H* unit was very different than a medical practice at Crabapple Cove, Boston General, or Mill Valley. The medical personnel had to learn that if they kept their focus on the war, they would not be able to effectively treat the patients. Their job was not to win the war. Their job was to treat the casualties of the war. This same perspective helps us deal effectively with the casualties of the unforgiveness war. The people God assigns us to help are casualties of a war that is bigger than you or me. The good news is the victory has already been secured, even though the battle rages on. We have to realize that if we focus on their wounds or their stories, we compromise our ability to help them and we may complicate their path toward forgiveness. However, if we focus on the cross and the freedom it brings, we can be confident we will help them be set free (when we walk in the Spirit). Listen to their stories in the same way a doctor listens to his patients. Listen to diagnose, so you can give them the help they need.

Along with a team of godly ladies, Toni has been ministering to a women's shelter in our area. The stories they hear from these abused women are heartbreaking, and the message of forgiveness is clearly needed. Each time Toni thinks she has heard it all, she hears a story that's even worse. At first, the ministry team struggled with feeling dirty after hearing the awful details of abuse and sin. Yet, because of the cross, we can never be contaminated by someone else's sin, even though it can feel that way. As believers, we are covered by the blood of Jesus and have been made righteous in Him. Nothing anyone else does can change that. So, there is no need to fear hearing someone's story. Any message to the contrary is a lie from the enemy of our souls. When Toni recognized this lie, she was set free to minister without reservation.

### DEALING WITH DETOURS

Occasionally, there are additional roadblocks to forgiveness when you are working with someone. The majority of the time the teaching from Chapter Two on Matthew 18 will unlock the door to their hearts and give them a desire to forgive. But if they are hesitant, help them understand that God expects forgiven people to forgive others. The Lord's Prayer in Matthew 6:9-15 is a great passage to help them see the truth that God connects His forgiveness of us with our forgiveness of others. With an overwhelming number of people, these truths are enough for them to choose to forgive. If you can focus their attention on the impact unforgiveness has on them, most people will forgive.

**Ultimate justice was satisfied on the cross.**

People will sometimes respond to the message of forgiveness with the question of justice. The argument is this: "There are certain things that require justice. If I forgive someone of these things how is justice served?" There are two responses to this concern. The first response is, *"The blood of Jesus covers all sins, including the ones committed against me."* Ultimate justice was satisfied on the cross. The second response is, God is God, and we are not. God is the judge who is ultimately responsible for carrying out all appropriate justice. Look at what Paul said in Romans 12:17-19: *"Never pay back evil for evil to anyone. Respect what is right in the sight of all men. If possible, so far as it depends on you, be at peace with all men. Never take your own revenge, beloved, but leave room for the wrath of God, for it is written, 'Vengeance is mine, I will repay,' says the Lord."* The bottom line is this: vengeance belongs to God, not us. God uses many ways to bring justice to a situation. He has established human government as one of the primary means to do so. Perhaps there will be a time to seek legal accountability or physical protection, however forgiveness offers the best protection from torment that will not go away, even if the offender is locked away for good. But rest assured, God will dispense His justice in all things, according to His wisdom. If we take vengeance into our own hands, He will discipline us as well. God is very good at His job and He does not need our help. To demand or enact further judgment is a declaration that we do not trust God. Not a good idea.

### ACTING ON A TIP

I recently spoke at a ministry center in North Atlanta. Through an out-of-the-blue circumstance, I was informed, just a few hours before my time to speak, that the leader of the ministry and her husband were scheduled to finalize their divorce the very next day. Toni and I met this lady several months before and had become friends. We had grown to love and respect her a great deal. She was not part of the speaking event, but I don't believe it was a mere coincidence that I had received information of their divorce plans just prior to speaking. After I finished my talk, I asked the receptionist if I could speak with the leader. She "happened" to be in the office and could meet with me. (It was interesting to hear later that this was her day off and she is rarely in the office on her day off.) It was a nice day, so we took a walk outside and sat on a short wall, in the parking lot, under some trees. Even though we have helped hundreds of people work through forgiveness, I was still hesitant to broach the subject, so I just blurted out what I had heard and asked the question, "How can I help?" We chatted for quite some time as she poured out her heart about her pain. In the middle of our conversation, her husband just "happened" to call. I heard her tell him, "I'm sitting here in the parking lot talking to

Pastor Bruce trying to decide whether or not I'm going to divorce you tomorrow. Do you want to talk to him too?" I'm thinking quietly, "God You are really good at this. Only You could create a set-up like this."

I began walking this ministry leader through the Protocols of Forgiveness. As we wrapped up this part of our conversation, her husband drove up with their son. The wife took her son to one of his activities while the husband and I began to talk. In the course of the conversation he forgave not only himself, but also some deep wounds from his past. The transformation in his countenance was remarkable. Then I coached him on how to love his wife even if she chose to go through with the divorce. By this time the wife returned, and the husband left for church. She forgave him, he forgave himself and she made a commitment not to divorce. They were reconciled—and a marriage was saved.

> Our passion is to see the forgiveness message become so natural in all of our lives, it becomes our automatic response both personally and in helping others forgive.

I believe the enemy of God wants us to believe the lies that say, "Live and let live," and "There are some things that just can't be fixed." The enemy would have loved for me to believe that when a marriage gets to the point of the final hearing with the judge, it is hopeless and you might as well not bother. Nothing could be further from the truth. The only thing that might have guaranteed this marriage was hopeless would have been for me to have not followed the Holy Spirit's direction to confront the couple. Had I not taken the initiative and the risk, had I disobeyed, not only would a marriage have ended, but also a vital ministry to women would have been significantly damaged.

There are situations, just like my ministry friend's marriage, all around us every day. Bruce Wilkinson has stated it this way: "All people at all times in all places are in need of a miracle. God has more miracles that He wants to deliver than He has people willing to deliver them."[10] He is 100 percent correct. I also believe the miracle most people need is a forgiveness miracle. Everyone has a wound. Everyone has been hurt at some time by someone. And a large majority of those people need help learning how to forgive. That's where you and I come in. We can help them.

What sets *Forgiving Forward: Unleashing the Forgiveness Revolution* apart from most other forgiveness messages is the emphases on people helping other people find freedom through forgiving those who have hurt them. Our passion is to see the forgiveness message become so natural in all of our lives, it becomes our automatic response both personally and in helping others forgive. God wants each one of us to participate in spreading the message of forgiveness to as many people as possible. I hope you are convinced of how important forgiveness is to God— that He expects forgiven people to forgive others. In fact, He demands it.

# Conclusion
▶▶

CHAPTER TEN

# Unleashing the Revolution

▸▸

ecently Toni and I had a chance to get away for a couple of days to celebrate her birthday. We planned to spend the night at a nice hotel on Lake Oconec that a friend of ours recommended. On our way, we stopped in Madison, Georgia to sightsee. This quaint town, full of antique homes, specialty shops, and a cute coffee house, is like *Mayberry RFD*, complete with picket fences and friendly people. Madison has one of the largest assortments of antebellum homes in Georgia. During the Civil War, one of the town fathers was friends with General Sherman's brother and managed to convince the General not to burn down Madison as he marched his army through Georgia.

Since this was an unplanned detour (the best kind) we began by visiting the Madison Welcome Center. As we walked into the old building that housed the Welcome Center another couple was walking out. We almost ran into them—literally. "Excuse me, ma'am. Thanks for holding the door, sir." And in we went. The lady manning the welcome desk greeted us, and I told her we were celebrating Toni's birthday. "What a coincidence. Did you see that couple? They flew all the way from California to visit

Madison for the weekend. Apparently it's her birthday too, and when her husband asked what she wanted for her birthday, she told him, 'I want to go to Georgia.'" Interesting! After receiving several tips on what to do in Madison, we gathered our pamphlets and headed out to find a place to eat lunch. That's when Toni heard Him. Walking down the sidewalk, Toni felt the Holy Spirit impress upon her heart that He wanted us to meet this couple. She mentioned it to me and said, "We need to keep our ears and eyes open." I'll let Toni tell the rest.

As we walked into the *Perk Avenue Café and Coffeehouse* to get a bite to eat, guess who was there? Yep, the California couple. *Lord, how do we break the ice with them? Please open a door.* It wasn't long before the California lady came near our table to get a better view for a picture of the inside of this historic building. She made a comment about her antiquated camera, giving us an opportunity to introduce ourselves. We shared birthday stories and good wishes, then she

> **She cried out to God, "Help me. Please send someone to help me forgive!"**

and her husband went on their way. I thought to myself, *that can't be it—there has to be something more to God's plan.* After our delicious Panini's, we headed out to tour our first antebellum home.

Guess who was the only other couple in the tour group of this 200-year-old house? The California couple, Bob and Robyn! An intimate tour—just the four of us along with the tour guide. Conversation became organic, not forced, as we walked from room to room. We enjoyed hearing their story and were amazed at some of the connections we had in the Lord. They were Christ followers—yay! We listened as Robyn shared some of the struggles she had at her workplace. Then we gathered together, held hands and prayed over her situation. It was beautiful. Grateful tears told us thank you. The tour guide just smiled. But God's plan was not yet complete.

As we walked together to the next home, God's purpose became clear. Robyn shared about a deep pain she had struggled with for years—an unrelenting pain with no relief. She began to open her heart just a bit when the large front door of the mansion opened for us to enter. Even though our conversation was cut short, I knew then why God wanted us to meet. After this, I couldn't fully focus on the tour because my heart pounded with anticipation as to what God had "up His sleeve."

As we walked down the steps of the final old home at the conclusion of the tour, I asked Robyn if she would like to be freed from the pain she'd carried for so long. Although I was a little uncomfortable asking her this, I knew, that I knew, that I knew, that God wanted me to—so in faith I did. "Please." she responded. I suggested we go back to the Perk Avenue Café for a chat. What happened next was remarkable.

Robyn began to tell Bruce and me that she hardly slept a wink the night before because of the torment she experienced. She cried out to God, "Help me. Please send someone to *help me forgive!*" After we shared some of the key principles, she wanted to be led through the Protocols of Forgiveness right

**"The only way I know how to describe my heart right now is—the shackles are gone!"**

then. As I began to coach her through the process, she stopped and said, "Do you hear that?" I hadn't noticed the song, *What a Friend We Have in Jesus* was playing in the coffeehouse. When Robyn finished forgiving and blessing those who hurt her, she again said, "Listen!" That's when we heard *The Old Rugged Cross* playing. She went on to explain that she plays three favorite songs on the piano daily: *What a Friend We Have in Jesus* and *The Old Rugged Cross* are two of them. Amazing!

# There is nothing more thrilling than to listen to the Holy Spirit, follow His lead, deliver His words, then sit back and watch the shackles fall off.

"How's your heart? What are you feeling inside?" we asked her. With tears in her eyes and a smile on her face she said, "I have been to Israel. I have seen firsthand what shackles look like. They are embedded in the stone walls and some in pits. The way they are positioned is painful for the person held by them. The only way I know how to describe my heart right now is—the shackles are gone!" At that moment, right outside the window of the coffeehouse, it began to rain. There was no rain down the street—only in front of the store. Everywhere else the sun was shining!

What an amazing encounter, and God had it planned all along. Who would have guessed that a day away for refreshment would lead us to a couple, all the way from California, who, for years, have been searching for relief—for the very answers we delivered. Only God!

A couple of weeks later we received the following email:

*Hello Toni & Bruce,*

*Just a note to say "thank you" for our time together in Madison. Knowing and trusting in how God works in our lives, I cannot say that our meeting in a small town cafe was by "chance." No, we were truly guided there to meet you folks, by His loving and gracious hand.*

*Instantly following our meeting, Robyn was able to let go of the pain about her mother; a hurt that she's carried for a long, long time. She feels free of the torment. Thank you,*

*Toni, for your kindness. I am very appreciative for now
having that portion of my wife that has been so occupied
with pain. Sharing that time with you and Bruce was a
blessing to us both.*

*We will continue to share your message of forgiveness
and bear witness to the Good Lord's direction in our lives.
And, with a fitting farewell heard often in our part of the
country, "Vaya con Dios—Go with God."*

*Bob & Robyn*

When touring old houses, we often hear, "if these walls could talk." Toni had this very thought as we toured those antebellum homes. Yet, right next to her was a lady whose heart wanted to talk, to be listened to, a heart yearning for freedom. We all have people around us every day who have that same desire to be heard and helped—and not judged. We have said it before; people are always safe with Jesus. They need to be safe with us too. There is nothing more thrilling than to listen to the Holy Spirit, follow His lead, deliver His words, then sit back and watch the shackles fall off.

Our prayer is for God to continue to raise up an army of people who will live out the principles of *Forgiving Forward*. Our passion is to see the revolution spread to every home, every church and every community on the planet. Anything less would be inconsistent with the Great Commission. Bob and Robyn have joined the Revolution. And so has Joan.

### JOAN'S STORY

We met Joan at a Divorce Recovery group we taught a few weeks ago. The following weekend she attended one of our *Forgiving Forward* seminars. After the seminar she waited until I finish speaking with everyone else and asked if there was a time I could meet with her. I said, "Let's talk now."

Joan shared with me an all too common story. After what she described as a 32-year tumultuous marriage, Joan's husband divorced her. She described the whirlwind of thoughts and emotions she experienced in the four-plus years since the divorce, particularly when she learned of her ex-husband taking another woman to some of the special places they had shared in their marriage. She remained involved in her church and had even become part of her church's lay counseling program. She had forgiven her husband, or at least had said the words several times, but she still did not feel free. I asked her, "Can you bless him?" She couldn't. "Then you haven't forgiven." I'll let her tell her story from here:

> *Bruce led me through The Seven Protocols. Heavy with emotion and tears, I forgave my former spouse and myself. I asked for blessings for each of us. Near the end, I realized I was puffing short breaths and told Bruce I felt like I'd exhaled for the first time in five months. I felt spent, but peaceful.*
>
> *Later I tried to think how I was feeling, going through the protocols and it came to me that I felt as if I had birthed each word from deep in my being. I knew it was important and thought I had forgiven both of us a long time ago. Thoughts and words over the lips don't do it. Only when it truly comes from the heart and we forgive as the Lord calls us to and pray for blessings for all involved, will we experience true freedom. Some of the thoughts continued over the next weeks and I reminded myself, as Protocol 6 directs, that I had already forgiven from my heart and prayed for blessings for both of us. Today I learned that my former spouse is getting married. I shed a couple tears, felt sad, forgave him and thanked my Lord for preparing me for this moment. As a lay counselor at my church, I realized how valuable these protocols would be for my counselees. Two days after the seminar, I was privileged to have this experience with one of them. There was an immediate transformation from relaxed to a painful facial expression as she dug deep, crying much and expressing her forgiveness for her former spouse, naming specifics. As she continued, freeing him from any debt and blessing him,*

*she gradually became more at peace. At the conclusion, she appeared drained, but stated she felt much better and there were fewer tears.*

*I asked that she take a moment and a few deep breaths. I then asked if she was ready to walk through the protocols again, forgiving herself this time—"Yes!" she exclaimed. We began anew. She continued to appear more at peace. She specifically forgave herself for each offense and asked for God's blessings on her. As she prayed, she had her arms crossed at the wrists over her upper chest; her fingertips seemed placed on her collarbone as though she were in an embrace. I asked if she knew what she had done with her hands. She did not. Two weeks before, she had shared with me how her mother showed affection with a very similar gesture when she was young. Surprised, she smiled at the thought and said she felt good. We hugged, smiled and shed a tear at the blessing of forgiveness from the heart!*

*A second counselee did not have time at the conclusion of our regular session to go through the protocols, but was excited at the prospect. I explained she could do it aloud by herself or better with an accountability partner. We talked of other family members that she needed to forgive. She planned to try it. A week later, I called. She had used the protocols and found freedom. She was very enthusiastic and said this was the tool she really needed and could readily use. The Protocols of Forgiveness are a gift that I have received and I will continue to share it!*

Joan is now an enthusiastic member of the *Forgiveness Revolution* and so are Bob, Robyn and many others that have been helped by this message. God expects forgiven people to forgive others, and people who need to forgive often need help forgiving. We all have been given the ministry of reconciliation. Our number one job as believers is to help connect people with the forgiveness that God has granted to them. We have come to understand one of the best ways to connect people with God is to help them forgive others. We have also come to realize how much fun it is to help people find freedom through forgiveness—people like Papa, Sarah, Emma, Phil and all of the rest of the people whose stories we have shared, as well as the hundreds we have personally witnessed since we have joined the revolution. It is just as exciting for us to see people like John, Joan, and Pastor Juan experience the joy of helping other people forgive.

Imagine what it would be like to be part of a family or a church community where people would automatically forgive. Imagine life and relationships without anxiety, depression, addictions, conflicts, divorces or church splits. Imagine the impact that kind of community would have on the people watching from afar. That's what our King desires His Kingdom to be like on earth. It's time for the Forgiveness Revolution to be unleashed. Will you join us? ***"Viva La Revolution!"***

# Notes

1. Thanks to Chip Ingram for this definition of love we heard at a ministry couples retreat, "A Joyful Journey: Experiencing God's Dream for your Marriage," at the Billy Graham Training Center at The Cove, Fall 2008.

2. Lewis, C.S. *Mere Christianity,* New York: HarperSanFransisco (1952) pg 115.

3. Wilkinson, Bruce. *You Were Born For This,* Colorado Springs: Multnomah Books (2009) pg 200.

4. Kraybill, Donanld D. *Willow Magazine,* Fall 2007.

5. Braun, Chris. *Unpacking Forgiveness,* Wheaton: Crossway Books (2008) pg 56.

6. Kittel, Gerhard and Friedrich, *Theological Dictionary of New Testament* (Abridged in One Volume) Grand Rapids: William B. Eerdmans Publishing Company (1985) pg 636

7. Reinecker, Fritz and Rogers, Cleo *Linguistic Key to the Greek New Testament,* Grand Rapids: Regency Reference Library (1980) pg 534.

8. Trent, John and Hicks, Rick. *Seeking Solid Ground,* Colorado Springs: Focus on the Family Publishing (1995) pg 113-114.

9. Wilkinson, Bruce. *You Were Born For This.* Colorado Springs: Multnomah Books, (2009) pg. 205.

10. Thanks to Bruce Wilkinson for teaching this truth at our church in Spring 2009. If you haven't read, *You Were Born For This,* we highly recommend it.

# Acknowledgements
▶▶

"We didn't know what we were getting into," is an overused cliché, but it certainly applies to us. We discovered the writing of a book requires much more than we ever imagined. There is no way we could have finished this project without the help of so many of our family and friends, as well as professionals in the publishing world. If we tried to list everyone by name that has encouraged us in this project, it might double the size of our book. But there are certain people we would be remiss not to recognize. So, we say a gracious thank you to:

Bruce Wilkinson, who first suggested that we write this book and then was unrelenting in encouraging us and introducing us to people who could help us move forward. Thanks for believing in us Bruce!

Those who helped us in the technical aspects of the project— Kathy Willis of KCW Communications for coaching a couple of rookie authors through the process. We learned a lot from you, Kathy. Chris and Alicia Gilliam, Jessica Cozzens, Ed and Ret Kosiba and Amy Hebel for your help in editing the book. It was unbelievable how much we missed. Thanks for your labors of love for us. Debbie Patrick of Vision Run for taking our manuscript and making it look like a book. Randy Drake for your amazing graphic artwork. You make us look good, our friend. Aldrich Lim for the use of your photo for the cover design. You are a God-send, all the way from the Philippines.

The ReGen Fellowship Church family—you saw God's hand on this message and released us to pursue it with great faith and generosity. The ReGen Leadership team—Ed and Ret, Jack and Virginia, Paul and Trudine; our hearts are astounded by the continual encouragement and support you pour over us. Our deepest gratitude to each of you.

The ReGenerating Life team—John, Kathie, Tom and Matt; we are so blessed to have you in our corner and cheering us on. What a journey we are on together!

James Hicks, for your seamless transition from counselor to best friend. Thanks for keeping our eyes on His Life. Martha and Kim, for your love, counsel and encouragement that keeps me (Toni) leaning into Him. Dick and Ann, for your prayers, encouragement and support that continually strengthen our faith. We are forever indebted to all of you, dear friends.

Our family—Papa and Mimi, Dad and Mom; we are who we are to a large part because of the love you modeled and shared with us. Kassie, Debbie and Mark, Ron and Kelly, and Sandy and Bob; we love you and would not have survived this long without your help and encouragement.

Our kids—Aaron, Andrew and Amy; thanks for hanging in there with us as we navigated through all the opportunities to learn the truth of forgiveness. We could not be more proud of you.

Jesus Christ, our Revolutionary Leader, whose death and resurrection paid for it all.

# Ministry Information

ReGenerating Life Ministries exists to take the message of grace and forgiveness to as many people as possible and to provide a ministry of reconciliation for pastors, churches, leaders, families and individuals. We accomplish this, in part, through *Forgiving Forward* Seminars as well as Forgiveness Coaching and Life Coaching.

For information on how to schedule a *Forgiving Forward* Seminar please contact us at: *seminars@forgivingforward.com.*

For information on scheduling Forgiveness Coaching or Life Coaching, please contact us at: *coaching@forgivingforward.com.*

> *ReGenerating Life Ministries, Inc.*
> *PO Box 1355*
> *Fayetteville, Georgia 30214*
> *770.461.4151*

Follow us on Facebook at *facebook.com/forgivingfoward* or through our blog at *forgivingforward.wordpress.com.*

# About the Authors
▶▶

Bruce Hebel is an international speaker with a compelling message that is revolutionizing the hearts of people from all walks of life. Raised in a pastor's home and educated to pastor the local church, Bruce is now following God's call to the Church at large. Backed by over 30 years experience leading churches, all of his training has led to this: total freedom through the power of forgiveness. Through ReGenerating Life Ministries, Bruce and his wife, Toni, are committed to bringing life back to the Church and its leaders through the power of forgiveness. Bruce is a graduate of Dallas Theological Seminary and serves as Adjunct Professor at Carver College.

Toni Hebel is a gifted communicator who serves alongside her husband and often speaks with him at events. She has been a guest speaker for various ladies events and retreats nationally as well as internationally. Locally, she's the associate director and a featured speaker at Touching Hearts Ministries. For over 25 years Toni has enjoyed teaching the Bible to women. She is passionate about helping all women find freedom while restoring their God-given destinies through an intimate relationship with Jesus. In addition, Toni is a skilled musician who has taught piano for over 25 years. Bruce and Toni live south of Atlanta and are blessed with three wonderful grown children who are all active in ministry.